The Art and Craft of
HANDMADE BOOKS

The Art and Craft of
HANDMADE BOOKS

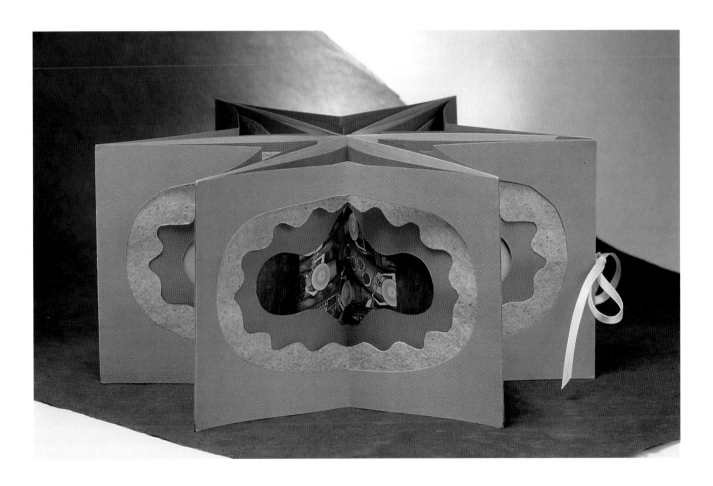

Shereen LaPlantz

LARK BOOKS
A Division of Sterling Publishing Co., Inc.
New York

AUTHOR: Shereen LaPlantz
ILLUSTRATOR: Tracy Aplin
ART DIRECTOR: Kathleen Holmes
PHOTOGRAPHY: Evan Bracken
PRODUCTION ASSISTANCE: Hannes Charen
PROOFREADER: Kim Catanzarite

Library of Congress Cataloging-in-Publication Data
LaPlantz, Shreen, 1947-
    The art and craft of handmade books / by Shereen LaPlantz.
      p. cm.
    Includes index
    ISBN 1-57990-180-8
    1. Bookbinding—Amateurs' manuals.   I. Title.
  Z271.L43 2001
  686.3—dc21

10 9 8 7 6 5 4 3 2 1
First Edition

Published by Lark Books, a division of
Sterling Publishing Co., Inc.
387 Park Avenue South, New York, N.Y. 10016

© 2001, Shereen LaPlantz

Distributed in Canada by Sterling Publishing,
c/o Canadian Manda Group, One Atlantic Ave., Suite 105
Toronto, Ontario, Canada M6K 3E7

Distributed in the U.K. by Guild of Master Craftsman Publications Ltd., Castle
Place, 166 High Street, Lewes, East Sussex, England BN7 1XU
Tel: (+ 44) 1273 477374, Fax: (+ 44) 1273 478606, Email:
pubs@thegmcgroup.com, Web: www.gmcpublications.com

Distributed in Australia by Capricorn Link (Australia) Pty Ltd.,
P.O. Box 704, Windsor, NSW 2756 Australia

If you have questions or comments about this book, please contact:
Lark Books
50 College St.
Asheville, NC 28801
(828) 253-0467

Printed in China

ISBN 1-57990-180-8

CONTENTS

INTRODUCTION

When I was an art student in the 60s, my class-mates and I wore olive green turtlenecks and made Japanese stab bound books for our haiku poetry. At the time, few classes on bookbinding were available, and the one I did take was somewhat uninspiring. The definition of a book in those days was static: it was something that looked like a library book, and covers were the only place to express creativity. I wanted to create objects with more personality, so I turned to other art forms. As the years went by, I kept the idea of making books in the back of my mind. I knew people who worked for small presses, and their work interested me, but didn't ignite my imagination. Finally, nine years ago, after exploring the medium of basketry for 25 years, I decided to try something new. That's when I rediscovered book arts. Incandescence happened.

In the years that have passed since my introduction to the field, an incredible movement has developed. Book arts is now a vibrant medium where creativity can be expressed through techniques, materials, formats, and content.

It's an exciting time to be making books. Artists are experimenting, pushing boundaries, exploring historical ideas, and applying familiar techniques in new ways. Technology provides invaluable tools. With a relatively low-cost computer system and a printer, it's easy to combine text and illustrations. You can now create images at home that in the past could only be made by a professional printer. Today, anyone who wants to make books can easily find instruction and inspiration. This book is a place to start.

WHAT IS A BOOK?

Ask yourself the question "What is a book?" Each of us may have a different definition. My definition is changing, but essentially I think a book must connect elements, such as panels or pages, and should follow a sequence. A newspaper has multiple pages, but doesn't feel like a book because the information isn't sequential, and the pages aren't all connected. A comic strip doesn't feel like a book. Although it's sequential, it's all on one piece of paper. Then there are scrolls. They're not multiple. Perhaps scrolls fit a whole different category.

ARTISTS' BOOKS

Book arts is a fairly new medium, so there aren't any rules yet. Since artists' books evolved from the tradition of bookbinding, many people think about them from that perspective: a traditional book has a set format, and the content of the book conforms to that format. Artists' books, however, are created from a different perspective: the focus is on the content, whatever it may be (illustration, typography, text, etc.), and the format, materials, and binding style are chosen to best complement that content. Consequently, artists' books feature more exposed and flexible bindings that allow pages to fan out in a partial circle, displaying the book's interior.

I believe there are six basic elements in artists' books: typography, illustration, page design (helping the viewer's eye to move around the page), text, binding structure, and presentation. If all six elements are blended together, they will enhance a book's theme, and in general, the book will be successful. Creating a book is a process: there's no right answer, only continued growth and creativity.

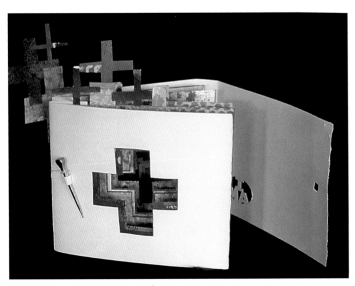

Ruthie Petty, *I Am*, 1999. 6½ x 7 x 1 inches (16.5 x 17.8 x 2.5 cm). Concertina; bristol board, business papers; water-color and calligraphy.

JoAnna Poehlmann, *A Clamor of Clowns*, 1990. 4½ x 6½ inches (11.4 x 16.5 cm). Concertina; board, rice and printmaking papers, ribbon; calligraphy, collage; rubber stamped and photocopied. Photo by Debra Walls

EXPLORING BOOK ARTS

Making artists' books is for everyone, from the pre-schooler on up. You don't have to be skilled at illustration. Clip art, collage, rubber stamps, prints, photos, and calligraphy are also great for images (please respect copyrights). Computers also allow us to manipulate a simple drawing into something more sophisticated, and combine it with words to make a page.

In this book, we'll explore seven different techniques for making artists' books: concertinas, slit concertinas, star tunnels, pamphlet and running stitches, tacket binding, Coptic stitch, and recessed skewer binding.

Starting with instructions for creating a basic concertina or accordion fold book, each chapter will build upon what you've already learned and introduce new skills. We'll also look at ways to combine techniques to create more complex books and explore new structures. Think of techniques as a vocabulary. The more techniques you know, the more you'll be able to express through your books.

The first project in each chapter will include a complete materials list, and you'll find suggestions for appropriate materials to use for the other projects and variations in each chapter. Use these suggestions as a jumping off point; the models are meant to inspire

you. Alter or adapt materials, instructions, and techniques to create your own designs.

This book also includes information on imposition (getting pages in the correct order), book mapping, parts of a book, and suggestions for book content. Not every book has to be blank—use your pages creatively.

Finally, to jump start your imagination, the gallery images in the book will show you some of the exciting ways that book artists are stretching boundaries and creating inspiring, beautiful, and thought-provoking books.

MAKE THE BOOK YOUR OWN

I believe in transmutation. That means adjusting your thinking, like your bindings, to fit your needs. The best definition of creativity I've heard came from my grandmother. She made art form owls into refrigerator magnets. Returning from graduate school at the Cranbrook Academy of Art, I asked her where she got the materials. She admitted that they came from a kit, but also that she had made so many *improvements* that the kit wasn't recognizable anymore. Please, make improvements. Transform artists' books into an even more vibrant medium.

THE BASICS

In this section, we'll review the vocabulary, materials, tools, and techniques you'll need to make the models and variations in the book. As you read, you may come upon terms that are unfamiliar to you. For clarification, please refer back to this section, the illustration on page 9 that shows the parts of the book, and the Glossary on pages 10-11.

Although we'll discuss a variety of terms used by book artists, please keep in mind that it's the book you're making that counts. It's possible to create a beautiful, exciting, fun, wonderful book without knowing any of these terms. It's equally possible to know all the terms and make an unappealing book.

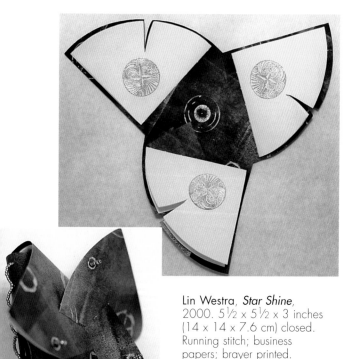

Lin Westra, *Star Shine*, 2000. 5½ x 5½ x 3 inches (14 x 14 x 7.6 cm) closed. Running stitch; business papers; brayer printed.

SIGNATURES OR SECTIONS?

Commercial printers don't read every page of every copy of each best-selling novel just to get the proper page order. Instead, little rectangles called *section marks* are printed on the back of each signature's spine. When the signatures are collated, if the section marks line up in a perfect diagonal, then the book's page order is correct. Commercial printers call the nested pages *signatures* (see figure 1-1). This term comes to us from medieval times, when scribes had to check for page order before binding. They numbered each signature as it was finished. To avoid second guessing, the scribe who numbered the signature also put his initials on it, hence the term signature (see figure 1-2).

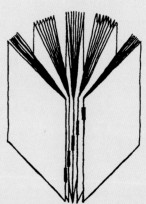

Fig. 1-1

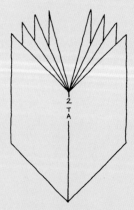

Fig. 1-2

VOCABULARY

ARTISTS' BOOKS: THE APOSTROPHE

The placement of the apostrophe in the term artists' books does make a difference. If we say "artist's books," it means more than one book by one artist. If we say "artists' books," it means many books by many artists, and that is the focus of this book.

SIGNATURE AND SECTION

The controversy over using the term signature or section to describe a group of pages folded in half and nested together has sometimes deteriorated into shouting matches amongst book artists. Select your favorite term and use it. With my foundation in the publishing industry and in graphic arts, I believe *signature* is the correct term, and will use it throughout this book (see sidebar page 8 for history).

PARTS OF A BOOK

As for the other parts of a book, the terms *spine, fore edge, head, tail,* and *text block* (or *book block*) will be used throughout this book. Just to make certain we all mean the same thing, take a look at figure 1-0.

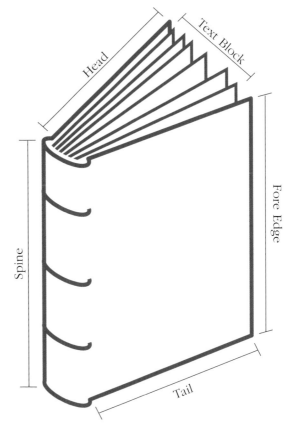

Fig. 1-0

Peter and Donna Thomas, *Pandora's Box*, Handmade paper, boards, wood; marbled, letterpressed. Photo by Peter Thomas

Susan Merritt, *1999 Card*, 1999. 4¼ x 5½ inches (10.79 x 14 cm). Concertina, business paper; letterpress printed, foil stamped and die cut.

GLOSSARY

BINDING. Refers to the basic mechanics of how a book is held together—the manner in which it is sewn, folded, or adhered.

BOOK CLOTH. Dyed and coated material, often paper-backed, used for book covers. The coating or backing prevents adhesive from "bleeding" or seeping through.

CODEX. The standard book format: numerous pages grouped into signatures that are then sewn together. Protective covers are added to both the front and back of a book in this format.

CONCERTINA. An accordion fold book. This style can be a simple book format, or combined with additional concertinas or sewn binding to make a more complex book.

EDITION. More than one copy of the same book. Editions are usually made to sell, trade, or give away. Holiday cards are an example of an edition.

ENDPAPER. Generally a decorative paper used to hide unsightly inside edges of a book's covers. When folded in half, end papers also attach a book's text block (see definition) to its cover.

FORMAT. The general appearance, shape, or style of a book. Codex, dos à dos, gatefold, and tetè â tetè are all book formats that can be bound using any binding technique. See also Formats (page 34).

HOLE JIG. A piece of paper with marks indicating where holes will be punched in a book's signature. This is an easy method of making holes line up for sewing or other types of binding. See also Hole Jig (page 69).

JIG. Any device, usually made from text weight paper or cardboard, that facilitates repetitious procedures. Jigs are most commonly used in edition binding.

LAP JOINT. A method for joining two pieces of paper by overlapping one onto the other. See also Lap Joints (page 23).

PAPERS.
See also Papers (pages 13-14).

Cover stock or cover paper. A relatively heavy weight paper available in stationery or office supply stores. It may also be called index paper or card stock. It comes in many colors, surface textures, and weights.

Oriental paper. A paper without a grain. Rice paper and mulberry paper are examples. Technically, this material is not a paper, since it is not made from a pulped fiber.

Pastel paper. A paper made for drawing with pastels or soft oil colors. It comes in may colors and several weights. The colors in pastel papers may fade rapidly. This paper lends itself easily to making hand-made books.

Printmaking paper. An absorbent paper used for printmaking. It comes in many different weights in both smooth (plate) and textured (vellum) surfaces.

Text weight paper. Basic office or photo-copier paper. This type of paper comes in numerous colors and textures and generally in three different weights.

Western paper. A paper with a grain, made either by machine or hand. It is made from pulped fiber.

Pam Barton, *Kapalapala*, 1987. 8¼ x 2 x ¾ inches (20.9 x 5.1 x 1.9 cm) Palm leaf binding; Tapa, acacia, koa, and raffia; relief printed. Photo by Clare H. Barton

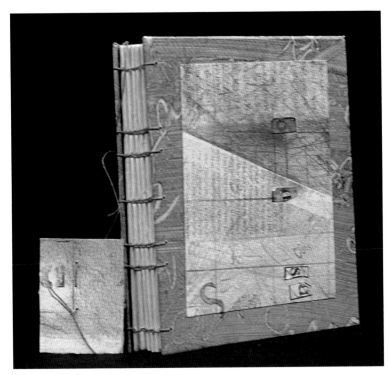

Jeanne Whitfield Brady, *My Book of Days*, 1999. 5 x 7 inches (12.7 x 17.8 cm). Coptic stitch; board, handmade and paste papers; mixed media drawing.

Judith Hoffman, *Celestial Navigator*, 2000. 11¾ x 5½ x ¾ inches (29.84 x 14 x 1.9 cm). Board and found objects; acrylic and collage.

PARENT SHEET. A piece of paper large enough to be used for several pages in a book. Generally, the size of a parent sheet dictates the size of a book's pages. See also Imposition (page 44).

PRESSURE SCORE. A technique that involves running an implement along a line to compress a paper's fibers. This allows for an easy, accurate fold along the line. See also Pressure Scoring (page 20).

PRINTER'S DEVICE. Also called printer's mark. An image, symbol, or logo representing a printer. See also Book Parts (page 72).

SEWING CRADLE. A device that allows for poking sewing holes in the spine or gutter of a book. Generally used with a hole jig (see page 69). See also Making a Sewing Cradle (pages 18-19).

SIGNATURE. A group or gathering of folded and nested paper that becomes pages for a book. In the printing industry, a signature is usually composed of four pieces of paper folded in half, making eight pages, printed on both sided to make 16 pages per signature. Artists' books vary in number of paper pieces or pages per signature.

STUB. A short piece of paper, usually the height of a book, bound in with the other pages of a book. A stub is often made from a heavier weight paper than the paper used for the pages in a signature.

STUB BINDING. Any binding that uses stubs. See also Stub Book (pages 98-102).

TAPE. A long narrow piece of material, usually fabric or leather. The long edges are finished, leaving no loose thread. A term now frequently used for tape is ribbon.

TEXT BLOCK. Also called book block. The contents of a book, excluding its covers.

TIP IN. Adding a piece of paper (usually an illustration, map, or printed piece) to a book, by adhering only the top edge (or in the case of stub binding, the side edge) of the added paper.

MATERIALS

Although the results are sophisticated, the materials needed to make the models in this book are simple. The section following discusses some of the considerations involved in choosing your materials. The term *archival* will be mentioned in relation to many materials; see the box on page 14 for more information.

ADHESIVES

While none of the projects in this book are held together strictly with adhesives, you'll frequently use adhesives for creating covers, joining combination structures, and adding decorative elements to your books.

Typically, the term *paste* refers to a substance that's primarily plant product, *glue* describes one that is animal product, and *adhesive* describes a substance made from chemical compounds. For the purposes of this book, the term *adhesive* will be used throughout.

See the section following for a discussion on the composition and attributes of commonly-used adhesives.

PVA

PVA, or polyvinyl acetate, is white glue, and yes, that means the white glue you can buy at the hardware, grocery, or crafts supply store. There are as many different recipes for PVA as there are brands. Some PVA is made for carpenters, and since 2 x 4s aren't supposed to bend, this glue is fairly brittle. Other PVA is made for fabric, which requires a lot of bending. The recommended PVA for bookbinding is made especially for bookbinding, and is available from bookbinding and some art supply stores. PVA crystallizes when cold, so if shipping is involved, it must be ordered in the summer.

Most PVA isn't archival (although some brands claim to be) or reversible (see boxed information on page

Diane Perin Hock, *City*, 1999. 6 x 9 x 9 inches (15.2 x 22.9 x 22.9 cm). Slit concertina, open; board, pastel paper, and telephone book pages, cut.

Susan Kapuscinski Gaylord, *Buddha's Path*, 1999. 11 x 15 inches (27.9 x 38.1 cm), open. Exotic and rice papers, board, beads; color pencil; photocopied. Photo by Peter Bartkiewicz

14 for definitions). PVA sets up rapidly. I usually describe it as a 30-second adhesive. It doesn't allow you to change or linger over the positioning of your materials. You've got to go for it.

I've heard that some studies show PVA to be toxic for people of small body weight (i.e. children), but it's still available at schools. I recommend treating it as a mildly toxic substance. Keep it off of your skin and wash frequently when working with it. Obviously, don't eat it. Apply PVA with bristle or sponge brushes. For large areas, consider using wallpaper spreaders. For small areas, I prefer to apply PVA by simply squeezing it from its container.

Wheat Paste

Wheat paste is technically called wheat starch paste, and it looks a lot like corn starch. It can be cooked in a double boiler, stirring constantly for 20 minutes, or cooked more quickly in a microwave (see recipe on right). Wheat paste is both archival and reversible (see sidebar on page 14). It has a long repositioning and drying time—hours or longer, depending on the climate. Unlike the other pastes, it dries clear and matte. If you're going to be making changes and second guessing your work, use wheat paste, not PVA.

Wheat paste is not wallpaper paste—that's like comparing apples and oranges. Bookbinders typically use a cooked wheat paste available from bookbinding and some art supply stores. It's essentially food grade, and is the only art supply I feel comfortable preparing in my kitchen. It does have it's drawbacks though: it attracts bugs. For those in a bug-infested climate or region, 10 percent PVA added to the wheat paste eliminates the edible quality, but you'll sacrifice the archival quality of your work.

I prefer using wheat paste when it's hot. It spreads like a dream and makes paper drapeable. Sometimes it makes paper act like plastic cling wrap. Unfortunately, hot wheat paste can be hot enough to melt sponge brushes, so use a bristle brush to apply it.

Either wheat paste or PVA can be used for any of the projects in this book. Try both and develop a preference. I prefer wheat paste for sheer paper or fabric, and in any instance where PVA will bleed through.

PAPERS

Most of us who make artists' books are serious paper addicts. The good news is that, with care, all the wonderful paper you find can be used to make books. See the Glossary for more information on papers (pages 10-11).

MAKING WHEAT PASTE IN A MICROWAVE

In a heat-resistant glass bowl, mix $\frac{1}{4}$ cup (50 g) wheat paste to $\frac{1}{4}$ cup (60 mL) water, and stir until all the lumps are gone. Then add 1 cup (240 mL) water and stir. Cook the mixture in the microwave for $1\frac{1}{2}$ minutes and stir, then for another $1\frac{1}{4}$ minutes and stir, then for 1 minute and stir, and finally, for $\frac{3}{4}$ minute and stir. Continue checking, stirring, and reducing the microwave cooking time until the paste is no longer white, but is completely translucent (the translucency means it's now wheat paste).

Cooking times will vary according to the quantity mixed and the particular microwave used. For smaller quantities, use the same 1 part wheat paste to a total of 5 parts water ratio and reduce the cooking times by half of what is indicated for larger amounts.

Types of Paper

For most books, the safest paper to start with is business paper from an office supply or stationery store. A variety of both text and cover weight papers are usually available. You'll often hear paper referred to in terms of its weight. Text weight paper frequently comes in both 60 lb. (27.2 kg) and 70 lb. (31.75 kg) weights. Just feel the weight and decide what you prefer. Writing paper also comes in 20 lb. (9 kg) weight, and is just slightly lighter. Some stores carry index paper or card stock (in between text and cover weight), which is a good weight for stub binding (see Glossary on page 10). Cover weight is generally the heaviest business paper available. Use it for covers, concertinas, or when you are going to print (with a typical ink jet printer) on both sides of your paper.

Pastel papers are used for most of the models in this book, and can be found in any art supply store. Pastel papers are colorful, but some of them are fugitive, meaning their color fades rapidly. Before using these papers in binding, consider what long-term effect this will have on your book. I use them for models, which aren't meant to have a long shelf life.

Sheer papers, and even lace papers, work well for wrapping signatures. If you want to use them for covers, they have to be pasted onto stronger papers using wheat paste, as PVA tends to bleed through. The paste should be applied to the stronger paper, and then, starting at one corner, applied to the sheer paper (this could be a two-person job). An alternative is to apply a paper backing to fabric, which will prevent PVA from seeping through and leaving ugly spots.

ARCHIVAL VS. NONARCHIVAL QUALITY MATERIALS

Most artists, including book artists, want the work they create to last over the course of time, so they look for materials that won't deteriorate. These materials are described as *archival quality*.

Not everyone agrees on the definition of archival quality. Some people say a slight acidity in materials is acceptable. Others believe that up to .05 alkaline value is acceptable (7 is pH neutral; a balance of acid and alkali). Still others say all your materials must be pH neutral. Check into the subject and make your own decision. You should know, however, that there's no such thing as partially archival. Also, remember that the term archival applies to all your materials, not just paper. Thread, adhesive, board, ink, etc., are either archival or nonarchival, too.

If you want archival quality, you've got to do extra work. If you use cooked wheat paste (see recipe on page 13), you must use distilled water to mix the paste, and prepare the mixture using only glass or stainless steel. Tap water contains contaminates and some cookware materials are also contaminates. I don't let any plastics touch my archival work for fear of contamination. I also work in white gloves to protect my work from skin oils.

Reversible is a word that is often associated with archival; it means your whole book can be taken apart and repaired. Even if a book is sufficiently archival to last 300 years, if it's not also reversible, the book will have to be tossed when the first disaster strikes. Mildew, book worms, moisture, and acidification are some of the factors that can cause damage to your book. Everything you do should be reversible so that you can "disbind" your book to repair it.

Text and illustrations should not be water soluble. Deacidification (the process of removing acid from or reducing acidity in a material) is usually done in a water-based solution, and your words or pictures will disappear from the page if they are water soluble.

Grain

Most papers (and even cardboard) that you can find in a stationery or art supply store have a grain, but Oriental papers do not. It's easy to recognize grain direction. Holding the paper up, gently arch it, then turn it sideways and arch it again. The arch made with the grain will be narrower and tighter while the one you worked against the grain will be a wider arch (see figure 1-3 and 1-3o). Folding with the grain is gentler on the paper and is considered to be the correct archival method. Folding against the grain is harder to do, and can break some of a paper's fibers.

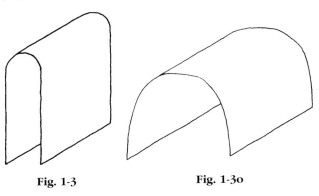

Fig. 1-3   **Fig. 1-3o**

BOARD

Many boards work well as covers. Four-ply museum board, or any other heavy noncorrugated cardboard will do. Check to see what's available at your art supply store. If you want to use archival board, make sure it's completely archival. Some boards are archival on the inside, but not on the two outer layers, or vice versa. When cutting heavy cardboard with a utility knife, use a cutting mat, and turn it over to avoid damaging it with the knife.

THREAD

Almost any thread will work for sewing structures. My preference is a plant fiber thread, particularly cotton or linen. Since paper is made from plant fiber, a plant fiber thread is a compatible choice. Most bookbinding supply stores carry a selection of linen threads. Pick a size (thickness) you like. Waxed linen stays where it's put, comes in many colors, and shows the Coptic stitch beautifully. Consider it for any exposed stitch. Cotton crochet thread also works well, and it comes in a multitude of colors and several sizes.

Julie Friedman, *Bride and Groom Keep House*, 1995. 4½ x 2 ½ x 6 inches (11.4 x 6.4 x 15.2 cm), closed. Foam board; gold, silver and copper leaf, paint, and collage.

Karen Page, *Untitled*, 1999. 8 inches (20.3 cm). Pamphlet stitch; polymer clay, pastel paper, beads, charms, feathers.

TOOLS

ost bookbinders use some of the following tools: a cutting mat, ruler, scissors, craft knife, pencil, and sometimes a hole punch (see the Basic Book Artist's Tool Kit on page 17 for a complete list). There are also a number of tools specific to bookbinding. You have a lot of options.

All of these tools are not necessary for every book, and as your involvement in creating books increases, you'll add more tools according to your preferences.

Jan Owen, *Juggler of Day*, 1999. 50 x 21 inches (127 x 54.34 cm). Concertina as wall hanging, open; acrylic, calligraphy.

SCISSORS AND CRAFT KNIVES

Many people are uncomfortable using a craft knife and prefer using scissors as a substitute. I prefer using a craft knife and rarely use scissors. Both are necessary. When using a craft knife (see figure 1-3a), remember to change your blade frequently, as the blades quickly get dull.

BONE FOLDERS

Bone folders are used for scoring paper (see Techniques on page 20) to create neat, crisp folds. They come in a variety of shapes, sizes, and materials (see figure 1-4). Find one that fits comfortably in your hand. Some bone folders come with a sharp edge (see figure 1-5). I find I lose control and make swirling, rather than straight, lines with these.

Note: Some people recommend wet-sanding a bone folder until it fits the hand and has a sharp point. If you chose to do this, make sure to wear a mask, as most bone folders are made out of polymer, and the dust created from sanding them is hazardous to inhale. Also, don't undertake this process in your kitchen, where the dust might have contact with food.

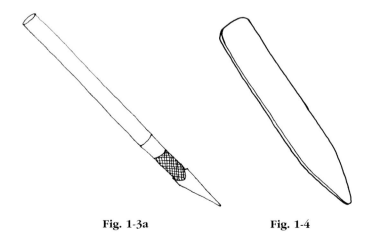

Fig. 1-3a   **Fig. 1-4**

Dry Embossing Stylus

Another option for scoring is a dry embossing stylus. This is my preferred tool. The small end gives a fine-line pressure score and is easy to control (see figure 1-6). There are many, many, more options. Find one you enjoy.

Hole Pokers

A pin vise is a traditional hole-poking tool for bookbinders. You can find this tool at a bookbinding supply store or a large art supply store, but they are usually relatively expensive. A frequent problem with this tool is that its pin continually comes out of the vise and has to be screwed in again. Sometimes this happens with every other hole. One alternative for poking holes is a ceramicist's sgraffito tool. The needle does not fall out, and this tool is considerably cheaper. Another option is a science probe from a university bookstore. This tool is even cheaper, and again, its needle will not fall out.

Needles

Always use blunt-ended needles for projects that involve sewing. After going to so much trouble to create sewing holes, don't poke new ones in your paper or board with a sharp needle. Sewing and fabric stores should have a selection of needles. An assortment of sizes from 18 to 22 should get you started. Once again, develop your own preferences.

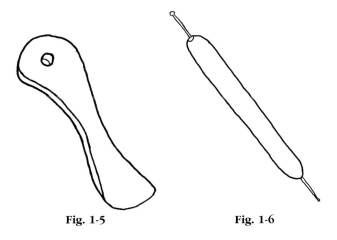

Fig. 1-5   **Fig. 1-6**

Basic Book Artist's Tool Kit

Before undertaking a book project, make sure you have a well-stocked work space. The following list of supplies and equipment can be assembled through a variety of sources, and some you may already have at home. If you have trouble locating any of these items, ask for guidance at an art or craft supply store.

GENERAL

- Adhesive (see Adhesives section to choose the one appropriate to your project)
- Bone folder
- Scissors
- Craft knife and blades
- Cutting mat or board
- Pencil
- Scissors
- Ruler (transparent or cork-backed metal)
- Adhesive brush
- Finger bowl
- Towel or paper towels
- Scrap paper
- Utility knife (for cutting heavy cardboard)
- Hand-held drill (for creating holes in heavy board)
- Hand-held hole punch (for recessed skewer bindings)

FOR SEWING STRUCTURES

- Blunt-ended needles (size 18–22)
- Sewing cradle (see instructions on pages 18-19)
- Thread (preferably cotton or linen)

Making a Sewing Cradle

A sewing cradle is a device used to create holes in a signature's fold or gutter, perfectly, each and every time (see figure 1-7). I learned the design for this cradle from book artist Artemis Bona Dea. It's collapsible, so it stores easily.

I always have my students make a sewing cradle during a week-long workshop. Although we also make between 35 and 55 books in those workshops, students frequently say that creating this sewing cradle was the most important thing they learned. Take the time and make yourself a sewing cradle. It makes that much difference.

Note: The measurements for this sewing cradle are generic. Adjust the measurements for any specific project.

Materials

2 boards,* 4¼ x 14½ inches (16.2 cm x 36.8 cm)

2 boards, 3½ x 6½ inches (8.9 cm x 16.5 cm)

8 boards, ½ x 3 inches (1.3 x 7.6 cm)

2 pieces of book cloth, fabric, or sturdy paper, 2 inches (5.1 cm) wide or wider

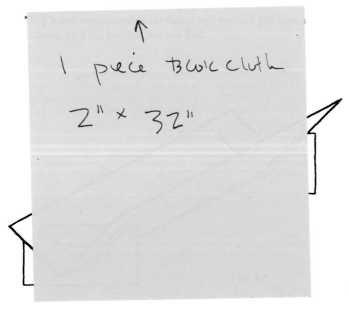

1 piece Book cloth

2" x 32"

Instructions

1 Select your board, and arrange the two large pieces next to each other with ¼-inch (6 mm) space between them (see figure 1-8). This space will be the joint in your cradle. A joint that size will allow your finished cradle to close completely for storage.

2 Adhere the book cloth, fabric, or a sturdy flexible paper over the ¼-inch (6 mm) space (joint) and around the edges.

3 On each board, measure and mark 1½ inches (3.8 cm) in from each side. Measure the thickness of the boards. Create two parallel lines that are the same thickness of the boards. These lines should be 3 ¼-inches (8.25 cm) long on each side of the joint, or 7¼ inches (19.68 cm) in total length (see figure 1-9).

4 Cut along the parallel lines. You'll be inserting the feet of the cradle through the slit, so the cut needs to be precise. Tip: It's easiest to cut boards with a utility knife (see Board on page 15 for more information).

5 The two 3½ x 6½-inch (8.9 x 16.5 cm) pieces are the cradle's feet. The eight smaller pieces are stops (see figure 1-10). These stops hold the cradle in place. All eight stops have to line up with each other. Accomplish this with a placement jig. To make the jig, take a sheet of scrap paper and measure and mark 3½ inches (8.9 cm) in from one

Fig. 1-8

corner, in both directions. Cut a straight line between the two marks (see figure 1-11).

6 Draw a line down the center of each side of each foot. The placement jig is a triangle. Line it up so that the long side of the triangle is at the top of the foot and the point of the triangle is on the center line you just drew.

7 Adhere one stop on each side of the triangle (see figure 1-12). The stops have to line up perfectly for the cradle to be straight, and they must butt up against each other, or the cradle will slip through the opening. Repeat for the other side of the foot, and for the other foot.

8 Slip the feet of the cradle through the slits.

9 To use the cradle, place a signature inside it, open to the center fold, then poke in the sewing holes. When you use the cradle, the holes will be in the fold each and every time.

If you're making a single-signature book with a soft cover, position the signature inside the cover, then poke holes through both at the same time. If multiple signatures are called for, use a hole jig to ensure that the holes will all line up (see Creating and Using a Hole Jig on page 69).

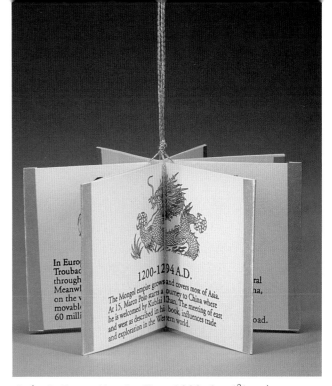

Cathy DeForest, *Hanging Time*, 1999. 3 x 4¾ inches (7.6 x 12.065 cm) Tassel binding; printmaking and decorative papers; screen printed.

Fig. 1-10

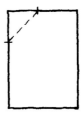

Fig. 1-11

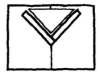

Fig. 1-12

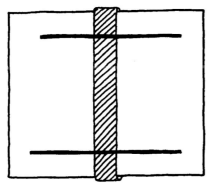

Fig. 1-9

Techniques

Even if you've never made a book before, you'll be able to create the projects in this book by learning a few techniques. Your skills will improve with time and practice. If you're an experienced book artist, you'll no doubt bring your own skills and experience to bear on any project you undertake. The information in this section touches on some of techniques used in creating the projects in this book.

Pressure Scoring

Pressure scoring is the technique used for creating folds, and will be used to create many of the projects in this book. Pressure scoring is a three-step process. First, measure and mark your paper. Lay a ruler on or near the marks—generally, about half the width of your bone folder to the side of the marks is best. Run your bone folder along the ruler's edge, pressing hard, to create the pressure score (see figure 1-12a). Without moving the ruler, slide the bone folder under the paper and fold the paper up (see figure 1-12b). Remove the ruler, and run the bone folder over the fold to make it crisp (see figure 1-12c). If you end up with a shiny mark (usually on dark paper), place a piece of plain, clean paper over the fold, then use the bone folder to make a hard, crisp fold.

There is another school of thought about pressure scoring. That school believes all folds should be made away from the pressure score, or the opposite of what has just been described. If one way doesn't work for your paper, try the other way.

Cutting

See the Tools section on pages 16-17 for more information on cutting tools. You'll be creating hard covers from board for several of the models in this book. When cutting boards, work with a cutting mat.

Punching and Poking Holes

You can create holes for sewing with a variety of tools (see Tools section on pages 16-17). For some book projects, such as those you'll see in the Recessed Skewer chapter, you'll need to use a hand-held hole punch for punching holes in signatures and soft covers.

Poking holes in heavy board can be a challenge. An awl is the traditional method, but it tapers too quickly for my taste, making all the holes slightly different sizes. An ice pick is a good substitute, but still leaves an unsightly, ragged mess on one side. A drill or drill press is the best solution. Hand-held drills are available in most hardware stores. The trick is to use a new bit. Old bits have dulled down and no longer cut through paper or board cleanly.

Applying Adhesive

When applying adhesive, always start in the center and brush outward. Brushing inward pushes adhesive under the paper or fabric's edge.

Adhesive gets on fingers. The difference between good and poor results with adhesives is a finger bowl. Wash frequently to avoid leaving adhesive fingerprints all over the book.

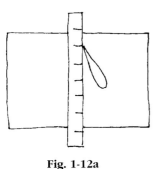

Fig. 1-12a

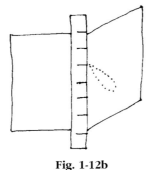

Fig. 1-12b

Fig. 1-12c

THE PROJECTS

Concertina

Concertina, or accordion fold books, are extremely versatile structures. This chapter provides instructions on creating a basic concertina and variations of the style. You'll also learn how to add features to the basic concertina to make more complex structures.

There must be as many different methods of folding concertinas as there are artists making them. If you find another method that works for you, use it.

Diane Maurer-Mathison, *Fantasy Gardens*, 1999. 4¾ x 6¾ inches (12.065 x 17.145 cm). Marbled paste and handmade papers; orizomegami, rolled papers; collage and calligraphy.

Basic Concertina

Almost any paper can be used to make a concertina. Printmaking, watercolor, and specialty papers usually work well for these structures. Text weight and rice papers tend to be flimsy, so if you use them, your book will need a protective cover.

Book artist Hedi Kyle taught me the folding method shown here. She says it's the only way to get perfect, even folds. I agree.

Mountain Folds, Valley Folds, and Lap Joints

Mountain Folds and Valley Folds

Throughout this chapter, the terms mountain fold and valley fold are frequently used. The following illustrations serve as a reference (see figures 2-0 and 2-0a)

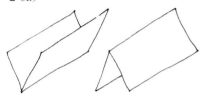

Valley Fold
Fig. 2-0

Mountain Fold
Fig. 2-0a

Lap Joints

Concertinas often require long strips of paper, sometimes longer than the paper available at art supply stores. Rather than being limited to miniatures, join two or more pieces of paper together with a lap joint (see figure 2-0b).

Simply create a tab the end of one piece of paper, fold it over the edge of the second piece, and adhere it in place. Trim a tab of equal size to the lap joint from the second piece of paper (the panels will then be the same size). Be sure to allow the adhesive to dry before folding.

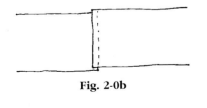

Fig. 2-0b

Materials

1 piece of pastel paper, 6 x 28 inches (15.2 x 71.1 cm)

Instructions

1 Fold your piece of paper in half (see figure 2-1). Open it out, making sure the fold points up, forming a mountain fold.

2 Fold the mountain to the edge (see figure 2-2).

3 Take the long edge and fold it to meet the mountain (see figure 2-3).

4 Open the paper and make all the folds into mountains (see figure 2-4).

5 Repeat the process, folding each mountain to the edge until you have created eight panels of equal size (see figures 2-5 and 2-6).

This model is an eight-panel concertina. If more panels are desired, simply continue the process, making all the folds into mountain folds, and folding each mountain fold to the edge of the paper. A concertina can be a book all by itself, combined with another technique, or enhanced with a presentation folder or box.

Fig. 2-1

Fig. 2-2

Fig. 2-3

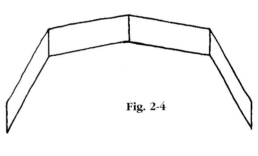

Fig. 2-4

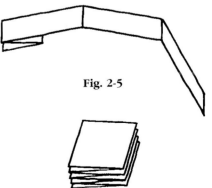

Fig. 2-5

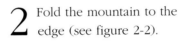

Fig. 2-6

Variation
Concertina with a Textbook Wrapper

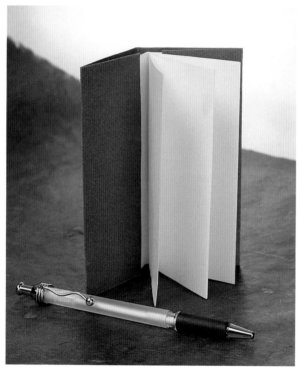

To add a textbook wrapper (remember high school?) to your concertina, open it so two panels are exposed, and place it in the middle of a piece of cover paper. Cut a rectangle ½ inch (1.3 cm) larger than the concertina on all four sides (if you've adjusted your sizes to make a bigger book, measure 1 inch [2.5 cm] around the concertina on all four sides). Measure the height of the concertina. Fold the head and tail of the cover paper to fit (see figure 2-7).

Measure the concertina's spine and score two parallel lines at the center of your cover paper. The space between the lines should be equal to the spine's thickness (see figure 2-8). Fold the cover paper to fit the concertina. Finally, slip the front concertina panel into the front sleeve of the cover and the back into the back sleeve (see detail photo, above).

Note: If you want more space for text, cut off the back cover's sleeve. This allows for text on both the front and the back pages of your concertina (see photo below).

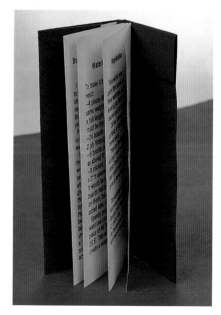

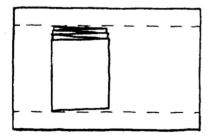

Fig. 2-7

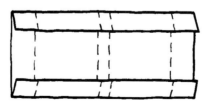

Fig. 2-8

Concertina in a Matchbox

A matchbox makes a great presentation case for a miniature book, and it's easy to make. Keep this idea in mind for use with any binding structure. You can personalize your book and matchbox with decorative papers, collage, rubber stamps, dangling beads, or gift tags.

Instructions

1 Using a text weight paper, create an eight-panel concertina (see instructions on page 23).

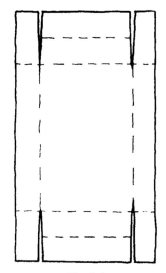

Fig. 2-9

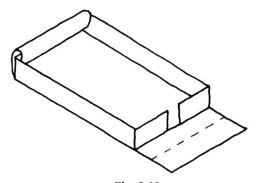

Fig. 2-10

2 Measure your concertina to determine the base size of your matchbox. Draw a diagram, as shown, using your base size measurement (see figure 2-9). Make sure the sides of the box are equal in size to the concertina's thickness. Notice that the top and bottom of the matchbox are twice the height of the sides. They need to fold over in order to lock everything in place.

3 Using cover weight business paper, cut out the shape of your matchbox according to the diagram and measurements.

4 Score and fold along the lines indicated in the diagram.

5 Fold the long sides up (notice that the ends of those sides are cut into tabs).

6 Fold the tabs under, then across the ends of the box.

7 Fold the ends up and over the tabs. Adhere each piece in place (see figure 2-10).

8 The cover of the matchbox is made from a single piece of cover weight business paper, and its width is equal to length of the box. Measure, score, and fold the height of the box's sides on the cover paper (see figure 2-11).

9 No matter how accurate your measurements are, changes can occur when you're making an object, such as a box. To ensure correct sizes, place the box up against the first fold of the cover paper, and score along each side. Next, place the matchbox against the last fold, score, and fold. Repeat until all the sides are folded.

10 Complete the cover with a flap. Its measurement should be equal to the height of the side of the box. Adhere the flap in place (see figure 2-12).

11 Adhere the back cover of the concertina inside the bottom of your matchbox.

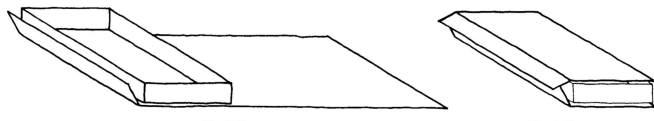

Fig. 2-11   **Fig. 2-12**

Inverted Concertina and Double-Inversion Concertina

To add more depth and dimension to your concertina, you can easily invert a section of its panels, and create new panels. The inverted panels are an ideal place to focus attention on stamps, collage, or decorative papers.

Inverted Concertina

Instructions

1 Create an eight-panel concertina (see instructions on page 23).

2 Pull back your first and last panels and reserve them as covers.

3 Create mountain folds in the center of each remaining panel. It's safe to start your mountain fold at half the width of the panel and 1 inch (2.5 cm) in from the head and tail (see figure 2-13).

4 After you've created the mountain folds, cut the head and tail lines of each, and pressure score along the vertical lines.

5 Invert the center fold, and fold both pressure scores backward (see detail photo, top left). Repeat the process for each pair of panels.

Variation
Double-Inversion Concertina

Follow the steps for the Inverted Concertina, but create valley folds instead (your outer folds will pop out, and your inner folds with recede).

Measure, score, and cut just like you would for the Inverted Concertina, and repeat for a second set of lines inside your fold (see figure 2-14). The outer lines get folded outward, and the inner lines get folded inward (see detail photo, right).

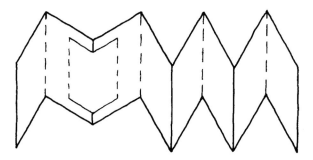

Fig. 2-13

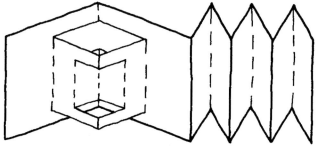

Fig. 2-14

Concertina with Pop-Up Panels

This model, one of my editions, features pairs of pop-up panels adhered to concertina panels. In the model, the pop-up section of the panels is flush with the head of the concertina panels, but the placement of the panels is your choice—there are a lot of options.

CONCERTINA WITH POP-UP PANELS

Instructions

1 Fold an eight-panel concertina (see instructions on page 23) from pastel or heavy weight paper.

2 Create pairs of panels from heavy weight paper. The model features three sets of panels. The size of the panels is your choice. In the model, the panels are the same height as the concertina, and their length is slightly shorter than a pair of the concertina's panels.

3 Decide on the placement of pop-up section of your

BESTIARIES

One of the most frequent comments I get in my workshops is "How do people find content for their books?" Historical approaches to content are an easy springboard. Let's start with *bestiaries* (pronounced beast-tee-aries).

A bestiary is a book about animals that may include quotes, myths, folklore, legends, or allegorical stories. Bestiaries are based on a second century A.D. Greek book entitled Physiologus, which was found in Alexandria, Egypt. By the 12th century A.D., bestiaries were used in Europe as a method of teaching Christian moral principles to children.

Challenge yourself to create a beautiful, meaningful bestiary. What character trait or moral principle could you illustrate with an animal: the industry of the ant, or the group work ethic of the bee? Consider your illustrating skills. Try using a children's book on animals as source material and make your own drawings. If you don't draw well, you can use rubber stamps or clip art for your illustrations. If you like writing, a bestiary can become a book of stories. If you don't, you can limit your writing to a simple phrase such as "The industry of the ant."

One very simple solution to creating a bestiary is to use quotes. In *A Bestiary* (Pantheon, 1993), compiled by Richard Wilbur and illustrated by Alexander Calder, each chapter has a title, such as "Grasshopper," one or two wire drawings, and a few quotations about the animal. Check your local library for quotation books that you can use as references.

Dorothy Swendeman, *Beastes of the Bindery*, 1996. 9 x 5½ inches (22.9 x14 cm). Lokta, leather, wire, plastic eyes, and business papers; block stamped and computer printed.

Various artists, *Bestiary: A Collaborative Book*, 1997. 8½ x 5½ inches (21.6 x 14 cm). Looped binding with tipped-in pages; various papers and printing methods.

panels. In the model, the horizonal lines of the pop-up are at the head of the panels and 1 inch (2.5 cm) in from the tail. The vertical pop-up lines start 1 inch (2.5 cm) in from the fore edges, with another line ¼ inch (6 mm) further in to create the pop-up. Measure and mark the position of the pop-ups on your panels.

4 Cut the horizonal lines of your pop-up section.

5 According to your marks, score two vertical lines for your pop-ups on each side of the panel (see figure 2-15). Fold the score lines, first up as mountain folds, and then down as valley folds (see detail photo, right).

6 Adhere the outer edges (not the pop-up section) of pop-up panels to the concertina panels. In this model, a single signature was bound into the fold of the last two concertina panels using a pamphlet stitch (see Pamphlet and Running Stitch chapter).

There are a lot of different ways to position pop-up panels. The following illustrations (see figures 2-16 and 2-17) demonstrate the different options I tried before settling on the positioning you see in the model. You can also create a pop-up within a pop-up, or place your panels asymmetrically (see figure 2-19). Experiment and chose the style that works best for your book.

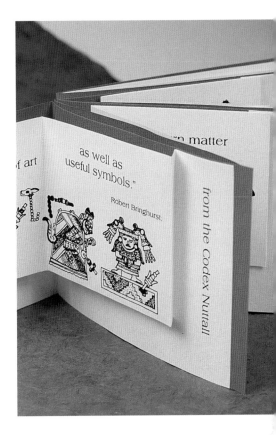

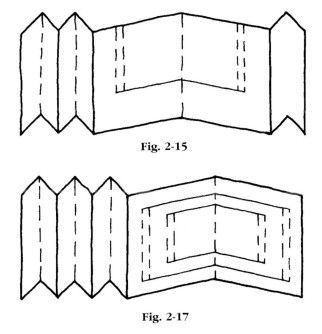

Fig. 2-15

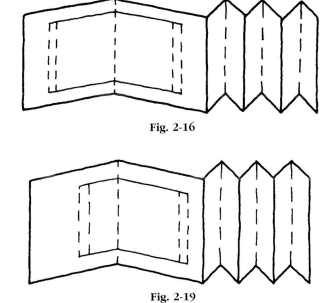

Fig. 2-16

Fig. 2-17

Fig. 2-19

Calligraphy Model

This model features a wrap-around cover with a flap closure. You can display this structure open or closed, and it's a perfect showcase for decorative papers or calligraphy.

Fig. 2-20

Instructions

1 Start with a long piece of pastel paper. Determine the size of your front cover, and measure and score the paper accordingly. The back cover is

the same measurement, plus the depth of the fore edge, plus the length of the flap (see figure 2-20).

2 Fold an eight-panel concertina in the center of the paper. The folds of the concertina will become the spine of your book (see figure 2-21).

3 Cut small pieces of decorative paper to fit into the center of each panel, and adhere them to the panels.

4 Create a 12-panel inverted concertina from pastel paper (see Inverted Concertina, pages 27-28). Tip: The easiest way to get 12 panels is to fold 16 and cut off four (the four extras can be used for another book). Position the inverted concertina before cutting off the excess panels to make sure your panels are long enough to fit into the model, and that you can attach one panel to the spine without positioning problems (see detail photo, top right).

5 Adhere your 12-panel concertina to the concertina you created in step 2. Its last panel will overlap the last panel of the first concertina's spine, positioning it next to the book's back cover (see detail photo, bottom right).

The closure on this model features a Chinese ideogram, $1\frac{7}{8}$ x 1 inches (4.8 x 2.5 cm). It was cut out of another decorative paper and positioned, then adhered to the front cover. Three sides were cut around the character, allowing the back cover flap to slip under it. The back cover is held in place with gentle pressure (see figure 2-22 and detail photo below).

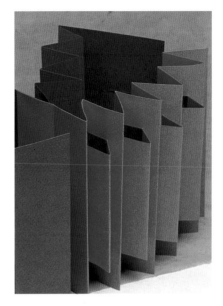

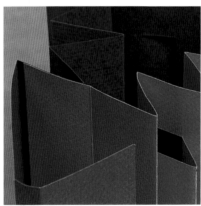

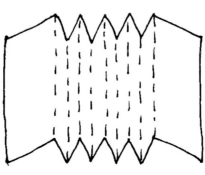

Fig. 2-21

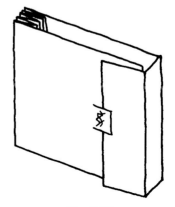

Fig. 2-22

FORMATS

Most books are created in a codex format, meaning they meet our standard idea of what a book looks like. There are other standard formats, such as those described below. Fortunately, almost all binding techniques work in any format. Trying a new format is just one more way to vary or individualize your work.

GATEFOLD (ALSO CALLED FRENCH DOORS)

Gatefold books have a spine on each side and an opening in the middle. Since this format shows two pages at once, it's excellent for compare-and-contrast books. It's also good for two intermeshing stories, or in a situation where two illustrations need to be shown at once (see figure SB 2-1).

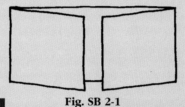

Fig. SB 2-1

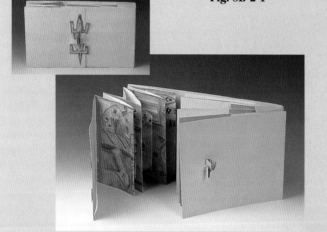

Gatefold format

DOS À DOS

Dos à dos is basically a Z fold (see figure SB 2-2) with a spine in each fold. This format is particularly good for two compatible stories, such as his and hers versions, or flora and fauna books. Historically, it's been used for two-part books such as the Bible (Old and New Testaments). It has also frequently been

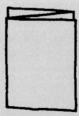

Fig. SB 2-2

used for bilingual books, with English on one side, and French or another language on the other.

TETÈ Â TETÈ

Tetè à tetè is a frustrating format for me. In his book on the history of libraries, *A Gentle Madness: Bibliophiles, Bibliomanes, and the Eternal Passion for Books* (Henry Holt and Company, 1999), Nicholas Basbanes lists the three basic book formats and includes tetè â tetè as one of the three. Before reading Basbane's book, I had never heard of this format before. Based on his description, I imagined it would look like the format shown here, but I haven't been able to find anyone who knows what the format really looks like. My version of tetè â tetè is good for love poetry and is especially good for weddings. The bride and groom can each have a side for vows they read to each other (see figures SB 2-3 and 2-4).

Tracy Aplin, *Model*, 2000. 8 ½ x 6 inches (21.6 x 15.2 cm). Tetè â tetè; cotton and straw handmade paper, business paper, dried flowers, and ribbon.

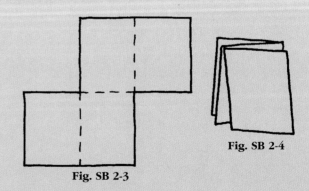

Fig. SB 2-4

Fig. SB 2-3

Gallery

Top: Marcy Johnson, *Book*, 1995. 6½ x 2½ x 2 inches (16.5 x 6.4 x 5.1 cm). Concertina; polymer clay, flax, and abaca papers.
Photo by Mary Ashton

Center: Susan Rotolo, *Music, Noisemaker*, 1999. 4¼ x 5 x ¼ inches (10.79 x 12.7 cm x 6 mm). Concertina; printmaking paper, found objects, board, acrylics, and ink.

Bottom: Liz Zlot (tiles by Sean Gouge), *Small Things Matter*, 2000. 5 x 3½ x 1 inches (12.7 x 8.9 x 2.5 cm). Tile, handmade paper, copper, wire, wood, board, silk; stamping; paste binding. Photo by John Lucas

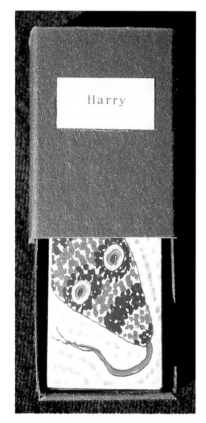

Top left: Dayle Doroshow, *Mind Map*, 1998. 2½ x 2½ inches (6.4 x 6.4 cm). Concertina, closed; polymer clay, millefiore and business paper; photocopy and collage. Photo by Don Felton

Top right: Sandy Webster, *En Garde!*, 1997. 8 x 3 x ¾ inches (20.3 x 7.6 x 1.9 cm). Rice and printmaking papers; block printed.

Bottom left: Jone Small Manoogian, *Harry Looking Out from His Matchbox House*, 1999. 2⅛ x 1⅜ x ⅝ inches (5.4 x 2.54 x 1.6 cm). Concertina, box; light board and business paper; color-laser printed.

Bottom right: Charles Hobson, *Man Ray's Kiss*, 1995. 9½ x 5 x 5 inches (24.1 x 12.7 x 12.7 cm). Metronome book; monotype.

slit Concertina

Take the concertina technique a step further by cutting slits in your panels and interlocking two or more concertinas. The slit concertina technique allows you to create books with a sculptural quality. Slits can be used as an alternative to using adhesive, letting you connect two or more concertinas with a clean, seamless appearance.

This technique opens up many possibilities. As soon as a traditional rectangular book is cut into different shapes, the book seems to float. It can become a paper doll chain or a beautiful maze of figures.

We'll start with a basic slit concertina structure, then look at different options for using slits to add interest to your books.

Dorothy Swendeman, *Carnival Cats*, 2000.
5⁷⁄₈ x 4³⁄₄ inches (14.92 cm x 12 cm). Slit concertina; business and origami papers, cut.

Basic Slit Concertina with Covers

When it's folded shut, this structure appears to be a simple book with pages.
Pulling open the covers, however, reveals a dramatic display. Simple slits cut into
the panels make it possible to combine two concertinas together, adding dimension
and motion to the structure. Notice that the concertina's colors alternate—that's
characteristic of this technique.

Materials

2 pieces of pastel paper (for the concertinas), 6 x 25½ inches (15.2 x 64.8 cm)

2 pieces of pastel paper (for covers), 6 x 3⅛ inches (15.2 x 7.93 cm)

Instructions

1 Fold each of the longer pieces of paper into an eight-panel concertina (see instructions on page 23).

2 Mark a center line in each panel. Cut along that line to the middle of the panel, creating a slit in each set of panels (see figure 3-1).

3 Open out the concertinas. Hold one over the other, slit sides next to each other. The mountain and valley folds in each concertina must be opposite those in the partner concertina (see figure 3-2).

4 Slip the two concertinas together, one slit fitting into its partner slit. This takes a bit of wiggling and feels awkward—that's normal.

5 Open and close the concertina to settle the panels into place (see detail photo, top right).

6 Fold the cover pieces in half and adhere them to the ends of the structure. Make sure all the edges are flush (see detail photo, right).

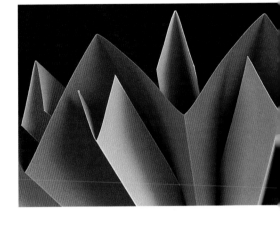

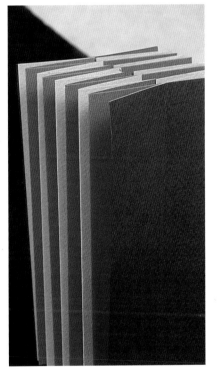

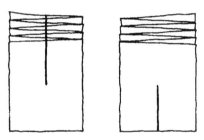

Fig. 3-1

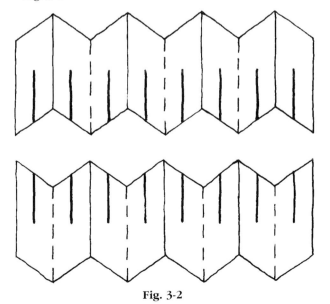

Fig. 3-2

Interwoven Slit Concertina

*Book artist Ed Hutchins designed this structure. In his original
model, the tabs on the taller strip adhered to the shorter strip,
forming connections. I altered the structure to create a slit
concertina. Feel free to alter any book structure to
incorporate your own design features.*

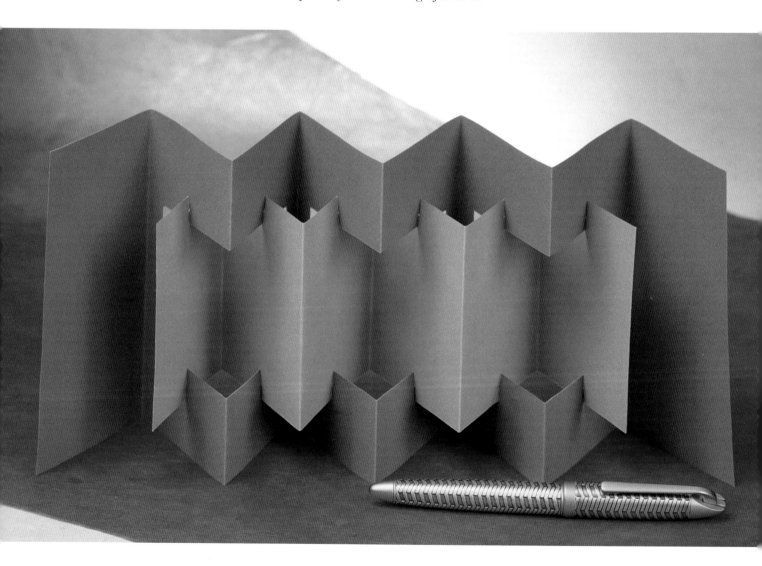

Instructions

1 Start with two pieces of pastel paper of the same length, but different heights. One should be approximately 2 inches (5.1 cm) taller than the other.

2 Fold each piece into an eight-panel concertina.

3 Cut two panels off of the shorter concertina (the two extra panels can be used for future books). You now have a six-panel concertina (short) and an eight-panel concertina (tall).

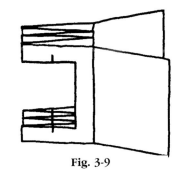

4 To create a hole in the center of the taller concertina, pull the front and back panels aside. The hole will be cut through the center six layers (see figures 3-6 and 3-7). To support the hole, the head and tail borders, or frames, need to be sturdy—1 inch (2.5 cm) wide is appropriate. There must also be a pillar at the back spine edge of the panels. The pillar should be at least ⅛ inch (3 mm) wide, but not more than half the width of the panel. Mark your measurements and cut.

5 The shorter concertina will float in the center hole you created in step 4. Cut ¼-inch

(6 mm) slits in the head and tail of the shorter concertina. These slits will be in the center of each panel (see figure 3-8).

6 Cut centrally-placed ¼-inch (6 mm) slits at the top and bottom of the holes in the panels of the taller concertina—the slits should be in the center of the panels, not in the center of the holes (see figure 3-9).

7 Slip the first top slit of the shorter concertina into the first hole's top slit in the taller concertina. The concertinas should be opposites of one another: one fold is a mountain and its partner is a valley (see detail photo, above).

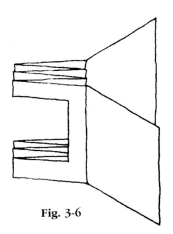

Fig. 3-6

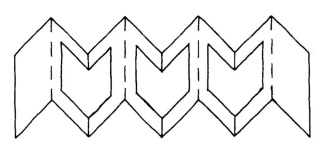

Fig. 3-7

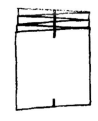

Fig. 3-8

Fig. 3-9

Continue working methodically, second slit to second slit and so on, until finished. Repeat the process for the bottom slits. Close the book and open it again to set all the slits and panels in place (see figure 3-10).

Fig. 3-10

Variation

Surfers and Sea Horses

The interior strip of your structure doesn't have to be a concertina. You can use pairs of panels cut into shapes, such as the ones seen here: butterflies, sea horses, and surfers (see detail photos, right and below). In this model, the sea horses came from clip art. The image was enlarged on a computer, printed out, and used as a pattern for the panels.

Cut shapes into the panels as you would cut a paper doll chain: fold a piece of paper in half, and start cutting from the fold, ensuring that both sides of your panels will be identical. Follow the instructions for the Interwoven Slit Concertina to cut slits in the panels and join them to your concertina.

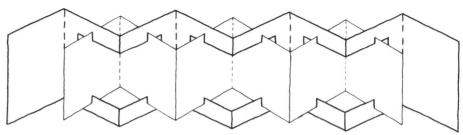

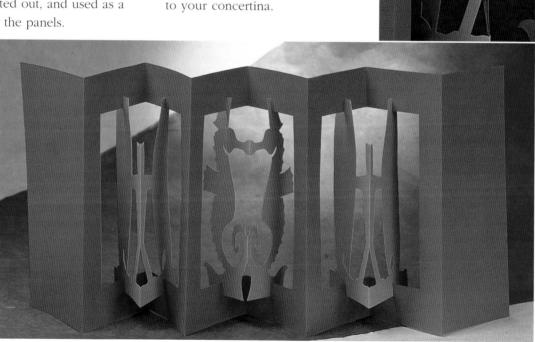

Variation

Geometric Panels

You can vary the shape of the holes you cut in your concertina, too. Create your slits in the same way described in steps 5 and 6 of the instructions for the Interwoven Slit Concertina (page 41), but alter the shapes of the holes in the tall concertina.

In this model, the hole in the center panel of the concertina is a circle (see figure 3-11). A rectangular pair of panels with a large central hole fits inside the circle (see figures 3-12 and 3-13). In the model, a smaller pair of panels cut into a circle is centered in the rectangle's hole. All three layers are connected by slits.

Each pair of panels inserted in the concertina's holes can introduce a new shape. The holes in the concertina panels to either side of the center are cut in swirling geometric shapes. In one of them, the paper that was cut out to create the hole is scored down the middle and adhered in the center of a rectangular pair of panels. The panels inserted into the final hole are cut in an intricate design that resembles a Chinese ideogram.

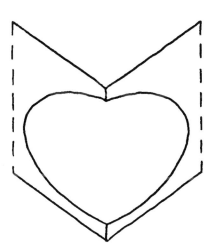

Fig. 3-11

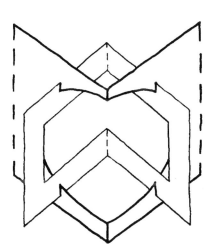

Fig. 3-12

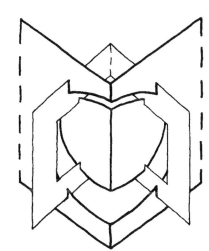

Fig. 3-13

IMPOSITION

When creating books, the word *imposition* takes on a new meaning. It's a term describing page placement—the way to get your second page behind the first page—especially if more than one page is printed, stamped, or lettered on a single sheet of paper (called a *parent sheet*).

Book design used to be so regimented that people had to memorize imposition patterns. In the past, a signature was always four pieces of paper, folded in half to make eight pages, printed on both sides, making 16 pages. The old rules don't apply anymore. Artists' books come in too many shapes and sizes. We can place any number of pages in a signature. If you use heavy printmaking or watercolor papers, one piece of paper per signature often works best. The opposite is also true. If thin rice papers are used, six or more pieces of paper per signature still work.

Whatever size signature you decide to create, you can ensure proper page placement by making a quick imposition model.

Cut a parent sheet the same size you're planning to print on. Fold it however many times you need to match the number of pages you want. For example, if you fold the paper twice, you'll have eight panels or pages. If you fold it three times, you'll have 16 panels.

Number your first panel, and mark it with an arrow to indicate which direction is up. You'll need to cut the bottom corners of your panels in order to reach inside the fold and number the inside pages, but don't cut any of your other folds. On your last panel, number and indicate which direction is up (see figures SB 3-1 and 3-2).

When you unfold your paper, you'll see that page eight is opposite page one, and so on. Follow the page pattern to create your book. If the pages are going to be cut apart, the model can also be cut apart.

If your project has holes in the binding or has pages folded and cut at odd angles, be sure to make a full-size imposition model. Holes allow you to easily slip one layer through another (see Star Tunnel Books chapter), but they also allow your under-layer to show through. If you're going to be placing text or an image behind a hole, you need to know the precise size so that both parts match up. You don't want to start adjusting the type and illustrations all over again because your hole is too large or too small.

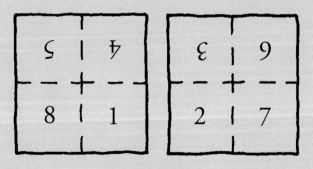

Fig. SB 3-1

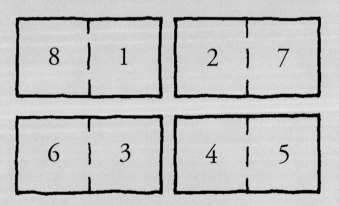

Fig. SB 3-2

Double-Layer Interwoven Slit Concertina

This book is another combination structure. Cutting all sorts of wild shapes and mazes for the interwoven portion of the book expands the visual impact dramatically.

Instructions

1 Create a four-panel concertina from pastel paper. Fold the center two panels into an eight-panel concertina spine (see figure 3-13a and b). Set this piece aside.

2 Using another strip of pastel paper, create an eight-panel concertina slightly shorter than your four-panel concertina.

3 Reserving the first and last panels for covers, cut holes in your eight-panel concertina, according to step 4 on page 41.

4 Now you'll create the interwoven portion of the structure. Using one or more pieces of paper, create pairs of panels. Cut the pairs of panels into geometric shapes (see detail photo, top right). Use any shapes you want, and combine panels from different colored papers, using adhesive or slits (see detail photo, bottom right). Just remember that the panels will float in the holes you created, so your final combination of panels needs to be 1 inch (2.5 cm) taller than the hole in your concertina in order for the slits to connect correctly.

5 Cut slits in the tops and bottoms of the pairs of panels, and in the tops and bottoms of the holes you created in step 3.

6 Slip the structures together through the corresponding slits in each piece. This structure is now the interwoven concertina.

7 You'll use tab hinges to fasten the interwoven concertina to the concertina spine you created in step 1. Tab hinges operate on the same principle as door hinges. They will keep the concertinas attached and prevent them from wobbling. To create tab hinges, cut a number of short, thin strips from sturdy, flexible paper (this book used 18 hinges). Your hinges will be grouped together in clusters of three, five, seven, or any odd number, depending on the size of your book. Try creating a practice model before you actually adhere the hinges.

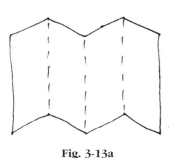

Fig. 3-13a

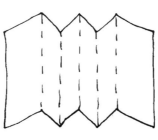

Fig. 3-13b

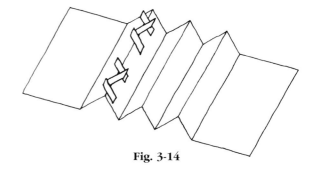

Fig. 3-14

8 Adhere a set of tab hinges close together, slightly in from both the head and tail of each available mountain fold on the concertina spine. The tabs will be on alternating sides of your folds (see figure 3-14 and detail photo, right). Carefully hold the interwoven concertina above the tab hinges while you adhere the hinges. Work methodically from head to tail, then move to the next mountain fold.

Tab hinges allow free movement of the concertinas in this structure. If the cover of the exterior concertina was adhered to the cover of the interwoven concertina, the undulating movement of the book would be lost.

COUNTING BOOKS

Counting books teach children their numbers. *How Many Bugs In A Box?* (Simon and Schuster Children's, 1988), a pop-up book by David A. Carter, is a good example. The book features wonderful pop-up panels and a progression of fantastic-looking bugs. Try creating a counting book of your own.

When creating counting books for adults, consider what you want to count. You may want to start with the number of vacation days you had and create a page describing what was happening on each. Or, consider adjusting "The Twelve Days of Christmas" to another holiday or time of the year (see photos, left and above right).

Elaine S. Benjamin, *12 Days of Halloween*, 1997. 5½ x 8¼ inches x ½ inches (14 x 20.95 x 1.3 cm). Printmaking paper; rubber stamp and lino block prints; hand coloring; stab binding.

I live in the northern California redwoods. If I made a counting book about my region, I would start with one trillium (a fragile forest flower), two banana slugs, and three Roosevelt elk. I would finish with a comment thanking the many dedicated environmentalists who work to ensure that there are still thousands of giant redwoods in our forests. What would you count in your region or favorite location? How would you end your count?

Another option is to simply illustrate each number beautifully. Creating content doesn't have to be complicated. Don't dwell on it—just do it.

Elaine S. Benjamin, *12 Days of Valentines*, 1997. 5½ x 8¼ x 12 inches (14 x 20.95 x 1.3 cm). Concertina, lokta; block printed and rubber stamped.

Gallery

Top left: Jackie Morse, *Joy: An Exploration*, 1998. 7½ x 6 inches (19.1 x 15.2 cm). Pastel and business papers, polymer clay, plastic tubing and ribbons; ink jet printed. Photo by Ron Bolander

Left: Charles Hobson (typography by Jack Stauffacher), ***Writing on the Body***, 1999. 11½ x 7¾ x ¾ inches (29.2 x 19.68 x 1.9 cm). Modified concertina with slipcase; printmaking paper; hand-colored photogravure etchings.

Above: Liz Tamayo, *Mauve Triptych*, 1996. 3½ x 1¾ inches (8.9 x 4.4 cm). Hinged concertina; polymer clay and canework. Photo by Donald Felton

Star Tunnel Book

Star tunnel books became popular in the Victorian era. Initially, the style was used for children's books. The deep panels, or star's arms, made it possible to create a vignette inside each layer, and each panel could be used for a different scene in a story. Star tunnels are still a perfect structure for adding dramatic visual elements and surprise.

The critical detail here is that there needs to be something at the end of the tunnel. Always add a visual. Canceled postage stamps, artists' stamps, or faux postage (see sidebar on page 66) were used for most of the models in this chapter, but rubber stamps also work well.

In this chapter, we'll look at several variations of star tunnel books, from a traditional structure to a tassel book, and two unique but easy structures called "The Interstate Highway Book," and my variation of it, the "Concertina Interstate Highway Book." In the final project of the chapter, you'll add hard covers to a double-layer star tunnel book.

There's not just one technique for making a star tunnel book. Be inventive. As the designer, you can adapt and adjust structures to fit your needs.

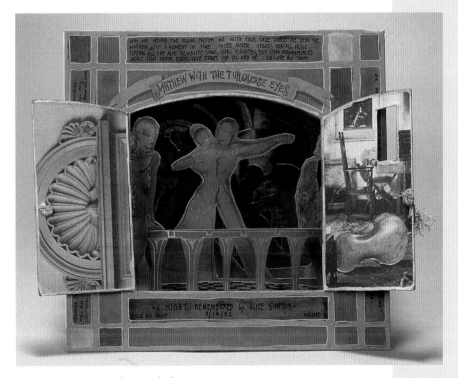

Alice Simpson, *Matthew with the Turquoise Eyes*, 1992.
10 x 10 inches (25.4 x 25.4 cm). Tunnel book; paper, watercolor; collage and gold pen. Photo by Marty Heitner

Traditional Star Tunnel Book

*This dramatic and versatile structure opens completely and features a
soft, collapsible spine that allows the front cover to tie to the back cover.
Three layers of eight-panel concertinas are joined
together at the fore edges with adhesive.
When the ribbons are tied, the structure
forms a four-armed star.*

Materials

1 piece of elephant hide or other cover weight paper, 6 x 31 inches (15.2 x 78.74 cm)*

1 piece of lokta,** 6 x 29 inches (15.2 x 73.7 cm)

1 piece of pastel paper, 6 x 25 inches (15.2 x 63.5 cm)

2 ribbons, each 10 inches x ⅛ inch (25.4 cm x 3 mm)

Decorative paper or images of your choice

*You may need to join several strips together with adhesive to get this length.

**handmade paper from Nepal available in art supply stores

TIP MAKE A QUICK MODEL OUT OF SCRAP PAPER TO CHECK SIZES BEFORE INITIATING YOUR PROJECT.

1 Make an eight-panel concertina (see instructions on page 23) from the elephant hide paper. This will be the outermost layer of your book.

2 Pull the two ends of your elephant hide concertina together to create a four-armed star. Try to get the arms evenly spaced. Measure the distance from one arm to the next (see figure 4-1). Add the four measurements together. This sum is the minimum length possible for the innermost concertina layer of your book. Tip: Make your innermost layer a little longer than you think it should be to cover any slight miscalculations. Your exterior layer is the longest and your innermost layer is the shortest. If your book has more than two layers, as this one does, any layers you add in between the inner and outer layers will have to be shorter than the exterior layer and longer than the innermost layer.

3 Fold the lokta and the pastel paper into eight-panel concertinas.

4 Mark your concertina panels to indicate the size you want your tunnel holes to be. Usually the innermost layer has the largest hole and each receding layer has a smaller hole (for example, in this book, the holes in the lokta concertina are smaller than the holes in the pastel concertina).

5 Starting at your valley folds, cut tunnel holes in the lokta and pastel concertinas. Set these pieces aside.

6 Nest all three concertinas together (the elephant hide concertina will be on the outside, the lokta in the middle, and the pastel concertina on top).

7 At each cover fore edge, place a length of ribbon or yarn in a corresponding position between the elephant hide and

Fig. 4-1

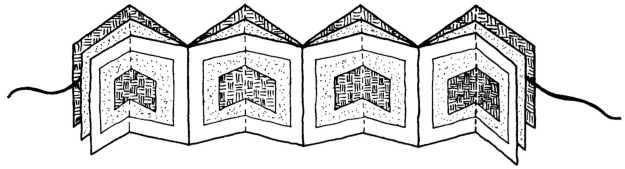

Fig. 4-2

lokta concertina layers. Join the fore edges of the two layers together with adhesive. The ribbon or yarn ties the book closed and also ties the covers together when the book is open (see figure 4-2).

8 Adhere the final layer of concertina to the two others at the fore edge with a thin bead or line of adhesive. The goal is to hold the layers together without interfering with the star's ability to open. It's also possible to sew the layers together at the fore edge (see pages 69-70 for instructions on the pamphlet stitch).

9 Cut images out of your decorative paper and size them to fit on the interior of your elephant hide panels (which will be visible through the tunnel holes in the other two layers). To make the images "float" in the center of the panel and pop out when the book is opened, they were cut shorter

than the hole opening (see detail photo, right). Size is critical. Try adhering a scrap image into your practice model to see if the positioning works.

10 Fold your images in half and adhere them to the elephant hide panels (see figure 4-3).

11 Adhere a decorative image to the front cover of your book if desired (see detail photo, right).

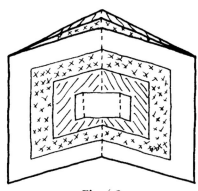

Fig. 4-3

Variation
Four-Layer Star Tunnel Book

This book has four layers instead of three, which usually means that you need to cut and fold one more strip. As an alternative, this book is made out of short pieces of paper, folded in half, and adhered at the fore edge (see figure 4-4 and detail photos).

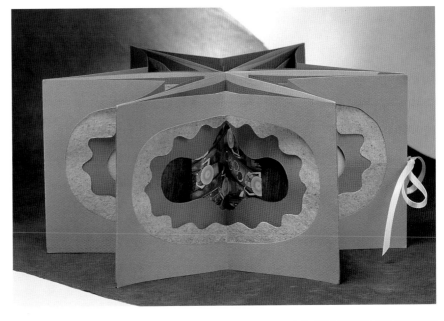

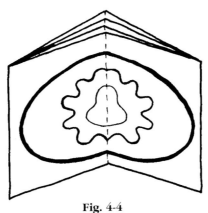

Fig. 4-4

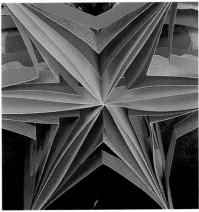

Tassel Book

I designed this binding to work with deeply embossed pages. Since the pages remain open permanently, it works well with thick paper, bulky collage, or tunnels. Each star arm of this structure has two layers of heavy paper, so you can also create doors and windows on the star arms. Just remember to put something behind them. You don't want to disappoint your audience.

Instructions

1 To make a basic tassel book, create a 16-panel concertina using heavy cover weight paper. Form a circle by joining the ends together at the fore edges with adhesive (see figure 4-6).

2 Select a yarn, ribbon, crochet tape, or heavy thread to make the tassel. Crochet tape (available at knitting or crochet stores) was used here. You'll need the crochet tape, yarn, or ribbon to be twice as long as the length of your concertina panels, and you'll use half as many pieces of crochet tape as there are star arms. This model has eight arms, so it requires four pieces of crochet tape. A six-armed star would need three pieces and so on. Place the strands together, and tie a knot in the center (see figure 4-7).

3 Lay the knot on top of the star. Carefully place one strand inside each star arm (see figure 4-8).

4 You'll need to make sure the tension of your yarn is snug between each arm. Turn the star over, holding onto the strand ends so they don't fall off. Even up the tension one last time. Tie all the strands into a knot flush with the top (see detail photo, right).

5 Add images to your panels. In this model, artists' stamps (see page 66) are scored and adhered to the center of each star arm (the stamp is adhered over the crochet tape).

Fig. 4-6

Fig. 4-7

Fig. 4-8

Variation
Six-Armed Star Tassel Book

This tassel structure provides a very interesting option. Holes are cut in the concertina panels, and pairs of panels (made from a text weight paper) with holes are adhered to the fore edges of the star arms. These two layers of holes form tunnels, so it's possible to see all the way through the book (see detail photo, right).

Start with a 12-panel concertina made from heavy weight paper. Cut holes in the concertina. Adhere the edges together to form a six-armed star. Use three pieces of yarn to bind the book.

Create six pairs of pop-up panels (see instructions on pages 29-31). In this model, six different colors of text weight paper were used (see detail

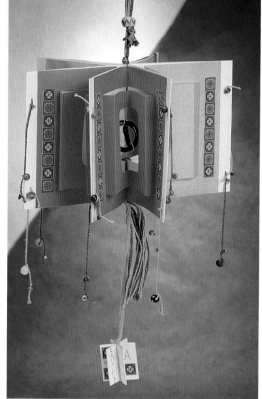

photo, bottom left). Cut tunnel holes in the panels.

Adhere one pair of panels to the inside of each of the star arms. In this model, the panels are not attached flush with the fore edge of the star arms. The placement is your choice (see detail photo, bottom center).

Adhere strips of decorative paper near the edge of each side of the panels. Using a hand-held hole punch, create holes near the fore edge of each star arm, and thread yarn through each hole (see detail photo, bottom center). If you like, add beads knotted into the yarn for a playful touch.

Echoing the style of the tassel book, a smaller book is used as a tassel dangling from the main book (see detail photo, left). Have fun with your books.

ABECEDARIES

W. Bory, *Alien Abecedary*, 2¾ x 5 inches (6.9 x 12.7 cm). Board and decorative metallic papers, and yarn; ink jet printed.

Michael Jacobs, *A Musical A•Be•Ce•Darian*, 1994. 15 x 6 inches (38.1 x 15.2 cm). Link binding; mixed media; laser printed with metallic embossing. Photo by Bill Wickett

From the old English word "abecede," for alphabet, *abecedaries* are alphabet books. They're the "A is for apple and B is for bear" books.

Abecedaries can feature any subject—flowers, recipes, sports—and can be written in any language or combination of languages. One friend, Dorothy Fenn, decided to use the language with the fewest number of letters. It's *Gamilaraay*, or Australian Aboriginal. Their words start with one of eight letters (b, d, g, m, n, t, w, or y). An abecedary in Gamilaraay strongly suggested illustrating the book with Aboriginal art, or at least in that style (see photo, bottom right). You can also make up a faux language, as Wadeth Bory did (see photo, top left). Since you're making the language, you're making the rules, and you can do anything you want.

In the last half of the 1800s, it was fashionable among certain religious or social groups to redesign the Roman alphabet, essentially creating a whole new alphabet just for the specific group. It should be easy enough to research this in the library, and the research could become an instant abecedary. Last summer I ran across *Deseret*, the Mormon phonetic alphabet. It was commissioned by Brigham Young, and used for all bookkeeping and church records. The alphabet never caught on, even within the Mormon community, but a modern-day foundry used it as a model for a computer font.

Another option similar to an abecedary is a *mnemonics* book. Mnemonics are pictograms that recall something to memory. Long ago, the inhabitants of Easter Island used mnemonics rather than an alphabet. Because their people were kidnapped and killed, there eventually came a time when no one remembered what memories the mnemonics were supposed to trigger. Unfortunately, their history and culture is now lost.

An abecedary of personal mnemonics, with a brief story for each pictogram, might be a fun project to create with your children. As a jumping off point, you could include memories of a vacation, of your dog's puppyhood, or of planting a tree in the backyard. Create a personal history.

The children's department of any bookstore should have many examples of abecedaries if you want to see other options.

Dorothy Fenn, *Gamilarraay/English Abecedary* (Australian Aboriginal), 4⅜ x 3inches (11.11 x 7.6 cm). Board, business and rice papers, ribbon, and clip art; color photocopied.

Interstate Highway Book

This is another structure designed by book artist
Hedi Kyle. It has since been modified and
renamed "The Slip and Slide Book."

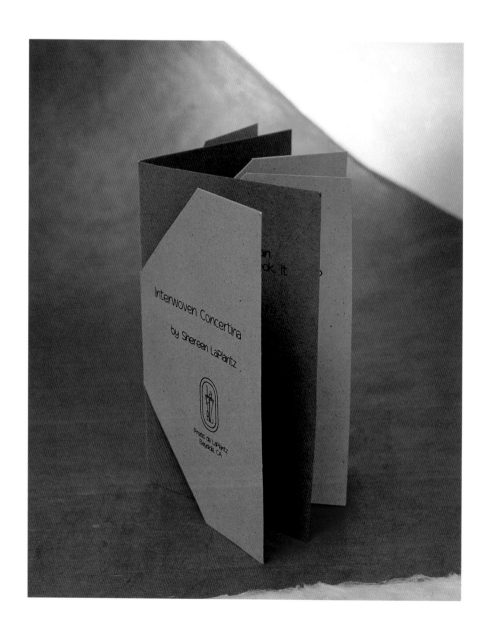

Instructions

1 Start with three pieces of cover weight paper (the model uses two light green and one dark green). Fold each piece of paper in half. Measure and mark one-third and two-thirds of the height on the spine of each piece of paper.

2 On one piece (in this case, it's light green), start from your marks and cut to the head and tail at an angle, cutting off the top and bottom corners (see figure 4-9a).

3 You will need to cut a hole in a second piece of paper (in the model, it's the dark green piece). Starting from your marks, cut a triangular or diamond-shape hole toward the middle (see figure 4-9b).

4 Curl one end of the first piece with cut corners (light green) into a tube. Thread the tube through the hole you cut in step 3 (see figure 4-10). This could be a perfectly functional eight-page book on its own, but this model takes it a step further (see detail photo, right).

5 Take the third piece of paper, cut its corners (as described in step 2), curl one end into a tube, and thread it through the hole. You now have two sets of pages threaded through the hole.

6 If you want even more pages in your book, add another piece of paper and create a hole in its center, as described in step 3. Curl one of the pages with cut corners (already in the structure) into a tube, and thread it through the new hole. This will add the new piece with a hole into your original structure. Repeat until the desired number of pages have been added.

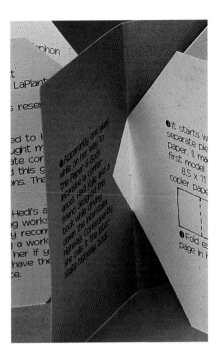

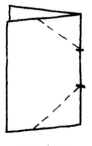

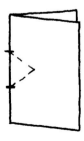

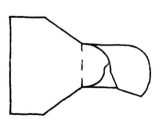

Fig. 4-9a   **Fig. 4-9b**   **Fig. 4-10**

Concertina Interstate Highway Book

This structure is my adaptation of Hedi Kyle's design. It features two layers of concertina threaded together in the style described on pages 58-59.

Instructions

1 Create a six-panel concertina out of parchment and a four-panel concertina out of pastel or cover weight paper. Tip: It's easier to make an eight-panel concertina and cut off two panels.

2 This book follows the same basic premise as the Interstate Highway Concertina (see steps 2 and 3 on page 59), except you're using concertinas instead of panels of paper. Your six-panel parchment concertina is your main concertina, and will have cut corners. Your four-panel pastel paper concertina is your center layer, and you'll cut holes

in it (see figures 4-12 and 4-12a).

3 Start with your six-panel main concertina. Select two panels with cut corners that are joined in a mountain fold, and roll them into a tube. Thread them through the first hole you created in your center concertina— "x" goes through "x" (see figures 4-12 and 4-12a). Repeat this process, threading "y" through "y." The panels have to be close together to get the tubes threaded through

the holes. The second hole may seem too far away to reach, but it is indeed the correct hole to go through (see detail photo, below).

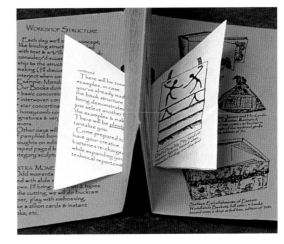

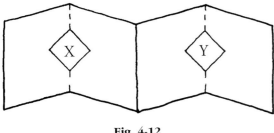

Fig. 4-12

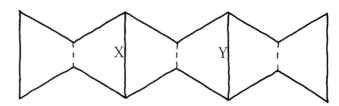

Fig. 4-12a

Creating Tunnel Holes

A tunnel hole is created by cutting a shape through the panels of a layered book starting at the valley fold (see figure 4-12b). Tunnel holes don't have to be round or square. They can be any size or shape you want (see examples on page 43).

Whether a hole is part of a star tunnel, or another kind of tunnel, some

considerations are consistent. Usually the first visible hole is the largest and the hole sizes become smaller with each succeeding layer (this can be adapted). The most important factor about a tunnel hole is that a viewer be able to see into it. Make a model before completing a tunnel book to make sure you've allowed enough light for a viewer to be able to see inside.

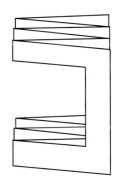

Fig. 4-12b

Variation

Single Tunnel Layer

This model is constructed in much the same way as the Concertina Interstate Highway Book, but there is a second inner layer of concertina in addition to the first (see detail photo, below).

Adding another layer makes it possible to add a tunnel hole and place an image inside it (see detail photo below, right). The second

layer is shorter than the main concertina layer, and has two extra pressure scores and an inverted fold in each pair of panels (see figure 4-12c).

Two panels from each concertina are adhered to each of the model's covers and artists' stamps are added for interest.

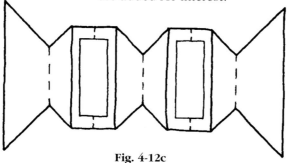

Fig. 4-12c

Double-Tunnel Layers
and Hard Covers

*When creating tunnels in a book, consider your light source. If the interior of
your tunnel is dark, a viewer can't see the image inside. One way to get light
into your tunnel is to use a light-colored paper. The outer layers of this model
are made with deep burgundy and chocolate brown papers. They're too dark
for tunnels. I used a light beige lokta inside the tunnels to add
light to the interior of the structure.*

Materials

For the book (text block)

1 piece of burgundy pastel paper, 4 x 25 inches (10.2 x 63.5 cm)

1 piece of brown lokta*, 4 x 17 inches (10.2 x 43.2 cm)

3 pieces of beige lokta, 4 x 3½ inches (10.2 x 8.9 cm)

2 pieces of beige lokta, 4 x 4½ inches (10.2 x 11.4)

5 artists' stamps, each 2 x 2 inches (5.1 x 5.1 cm)

For the covers

2 pieces of board, 4 x 3⅛ inches (10.2 x 7.93 cm)

2 pieces of brown lokta, 6 x 5⅛ inches (15.2 x 13 cm)

2 pieces of burgundy pastel paper, 3⅝ x 2⅞ inches (9.20 x 7.30 cm)

2 pieces of ribbon, ⅛ inch x 10 inches (3 mm x 25.4 cm)

*handmade paper from Nepal

Instructions

For the book (text block)

1 Pressure score and fold your pastel paper, and cut holes in your panels (see figure 4-15).

2 Pressure score and invert the fold in your panels (see figure 4-16 and instructions for Inverted Concertina on page 28). This allows you to have tunnels inside the panels.

3 Repeat this process (pressure score, fold, pressure score again, and invert your folds) on the brown lokta strip, and then cut the corners of your panels (see figures 4-15 and 4-16). If you're adjusting this model to a different size, plan on making several scrap paper models first to make sure everything matches up.

4 Roll the lokta into a tube and thread it through the hole in the pastel paper (see step 4 on page 59).

5 Adhere the artists' stamps to the small beige pieces of lokta. Fold the lokta pieces in half. Put a bead of adhesive on each fore edge. Slip each lokta piece inside each tunnel hole (see detail photo, right). Finger press to make the adhesive stick. It's a lot easier than it sounds.

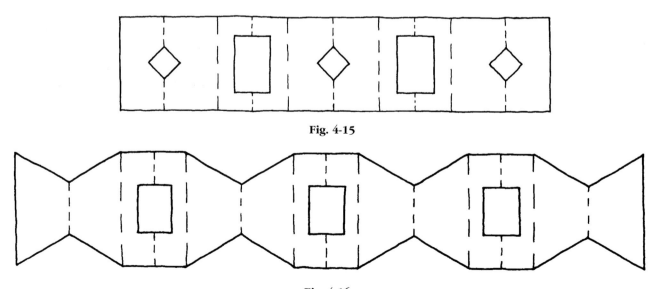

Fig. 4-15

Fig. 4-16

For the covers

Hard covers protect a book and can be added to most structures. Covers are usually a little bit larger than text blocks to prevent the pages from abrading, but that doesn't work with concertinas (including star tunnels) or any book structure that's displayed open. Larger covers cause a book to tip forward at an angle.

6 Cut the covers flush with (the same size as) the text block (book).

7 Boards usually aren't attractive, but you can cover them with something more

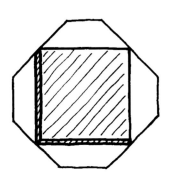

Fig. 4-17

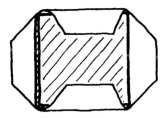

Fig. 4-18

appealing. Fabric, book cloth, or any paper that withstands abrasion are all good choices for cover paper. Cut your cover paper (in this case the lokta), allowing about 1 inch (2.5 cm) of extra space on all four sides.

8 Apply adhesive to the lokta. Position your board. It must line up perfectly with your corner cuts.

9 Wait until now to trim your corners, and trim them at a diagonal (see figure 4-17). It's sticky and messy, but the alignment will be perfect.

10 Fold the head and tail over. Since adhesive has been applied to both, they'll stick to the board (see figure 4-18).

11 Finally, wrap the sides around and press them in place. Repeat this process for the other cover.

12 Mark the cover's fore edge at the center, and

position your ribbons at the mark. Try to get your front and back cover ribbons to line up (doing so makes it easier to tie a bow). Using adhesive, attach the two ribbons, one inside each cover. In order to keep the ribbons anchored, make sure they're positioned far enough inside the covers (see figure 4-19).

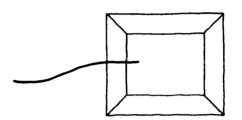

Fig. 4-19

13 Attach the book to the covers by adhering the cut-corner lokta pieces to the inside of the covers (see detail photos, left and right). Be sure to position the edge of each cover flush with the spine, or the book will be askew.

14 Use the remaining two pieces of pastel paper as endpaper. Center and adhere them inside the covers. They will cover up the mess.

FAUX POSTAGE AND ARTISTS' STAMPS

The term *faux postage* describes miniature pieces of simple art in the shape and style of postage stamps. Artists' stamps, also called *artistamps*, are similar to faux postage but are more complex and look less like real postage. As I understand the law, it's illegal to create something that could be mistaken for real postage. When designing stamps, remember that not everyone is observant. Design something that cannot be mistaken for an official stamp.

Faux postage often has a name; mine is LaPlantz Post. It can also have the name of a fantasy country and an unusual denomination, such as 49 cents. Artists' stamps allow you to use your imagination; they're not meant to look like real postage. They can be fun, quick formats for exploring graphic design, typography, color schemes, or illustration techniques. You can create something that is a combination of both techniques; since these are new media, there hasn't been much time to develop a vocabulary and definitions.

Gummed paper for stamps is available at wholesale office paper supply stores, or check with your local printer. Your printer might also have a perforator, but it's unlikely. Preperforated gummed paper is also available,

but it's difficult to find. Check with rubber stamp stores in your area to see if they carry it. It's more likely that you'll have to turn to a big rubber stamp company to find it. Rubber stamp stores usually carry rubber stamps shaped like the outlines of postage. It's also possible to make dotted lines on an illustration using a computer program, and design inside the dots.

Faux postage and artists' stamps are great images to put on pages, inside tunnels, and behind windows. They are a fun piece of *lagniappe* (a French word for "a little something extra"). Design one for each new book and send them out with the book. They can even be sent out as advertising for a business, event, or anything else you want to let people know about.

Shereen LaPlantz, *Artists' Stamps & Faux Postage*, 2000. Images from medieval manuscripts, ink jet printed on contact paper.

Gallery

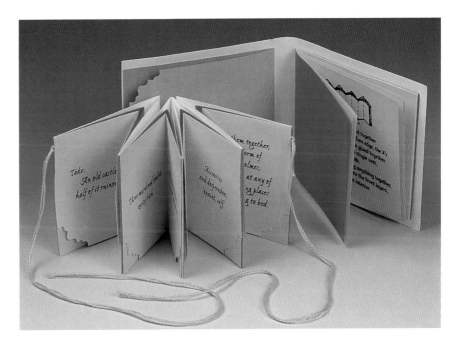

Top left: Ann Vicente, *Vancouver Summer*, 1997. 8 x 15 x 8 inches (20.3 x 38.1 x 20.3 cm). Tunnel book, open; handmade paper; calligraphy.

Center left: Melissa Dinwiddie, *Alphabet Book*, 1997. 2⅛ x 2⅝ x 1 inches (5.39 x 6.66 x 2.5 cm). Concertina star tunnel with piano hinge spine, closed; pastel and printmaking papers; toothpick; hand-cut images.

Center right: C.J Grossman, *Cuba Con Limon*, 1999. 8½ x 5¾ x 6½ inches (21.6 x 14.6 x 16.5 cm). Tunnel with concertina sides; paper; photo transfers. Photo by Sibila Savage

Right: Shereen LaPlantz, *Star Tunnel Books*, 1998. 3¾ x 4 inches (9.5 x 10.20 cm). Printmaking and business papers with manila envelope; photocopied.

Pamphlet and Running Stitch

So far in this book, we've explored many variations and combinations of books that fold. Now our focus shifts to books with stitched or sewn bindings. The bindings you'll see in the next four chapters all involve some kind of threading, sewing or stitching, and feature exposed bindings.

Pamphlet and running stitches are two of the most basic binding stitches. They're great any time you create a book with a single signature. Single signatures can be tucked into any fold with one of these stitches, and if you have a lot of folds, you can create a lot of signatures. These two stitches are also fast. If you get a wild idea today and want to bind a quick edition tomorrow, a pamphlet or running stitch is a good solution.

A sturdy thread is appropriate for the pamphlet stitch. Anything that's not elastic, such as embroidery or sewing thread, cotton crochet tape, or linen binder's thread will work.

Lynne Perrella, *Open Book*, 1997. 12 x 16 x 4 inches (30.5 x 40.6 x 10.2 cm). Mixed media, photocopy transfers, and collage. Photo by Pig Farm Photos

Basic Pamphlet Stitch Book

The basic pamphlet stitch is commonly used for books with single-signature bindings and soft covers. If you start your sewing on the outside, your knot will be on the outside. This allows you to attach beads, charms, and other dangling objects to your thread ends. Likewise, if you start sewing on the inside, your knot will be on the inside.

Making and Using a Hole Jig

For any structures that require sewing (including the books in this chapter), you'll need a hole jig to ensure that all your holes are in the places you want them to be, and that holes line up when you're using a cover, or more than one signature in a book.

To create a hole jig, take a scrap of paper and cut it to the height of your book, signature, or cover (whatever you're poking holes in). It should be at least 2 inches (5.1 cm) wide. Since this is just a scrap of paper, don't worry if it doesn't look pretty.

Fold the hole jig in half lengthwise. Center your signature, cover, or both, together in the jig, and measure where you want your holes to be. Mark the places you want the holes to be on your jig, then poke your holes.

If you're going to create a multisignature structure, use your sewing cradle (see pages 18-19) for this procedure. Lay your signature in the cradle, position the hole jig on top of it, measure, mark, and poke your holes.

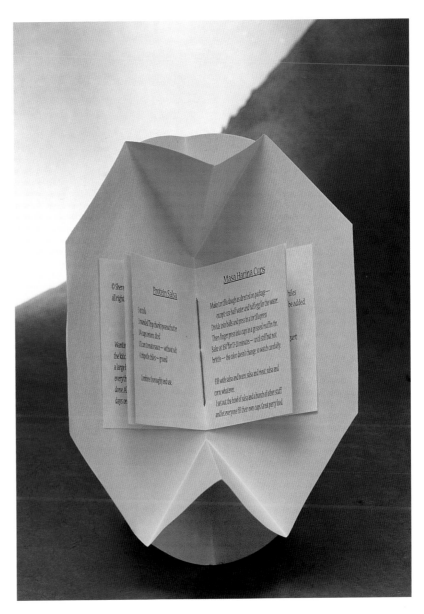

Materials

1 circular piece of light-colored cover weight paper, 8-inch (20.3 cm) diameter

1 piece of green text weight paper, 8½ x 8½ inches (21.6 x 21.6 cm)

3 pieces of parchment (text weight) paper, 6 x 3 inches (15.2 x 7.6 cm)

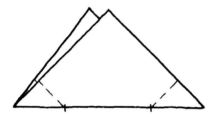

Fig. 5-1

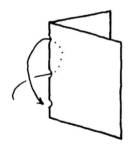

Fig. 5-2

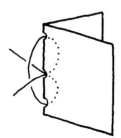

Fig. 5-3

Instructions

1 In this model, the cover is a piece of cover weight paper cut into a circle and folded down the center.

2 Inside the cover, the green text weight page is folded in half diagonally to create a simple explosion page (see instructions on page 78). Score the explosion page down the middle and in diagonals on the side so it folds in when the book is closed (see figure 5-1). Set this piece aside—you won't adhere this layer until after you've done your stitching.

3 A small signature of three text weight pages (folded once) is centered in the fold of the two outer layers.

4 Measure, mark, and poke three holes in your signature, using your hole jig (see page 69). Center the signature, aligning it with your explosion page, and poke corresponding holes through both pieces.

5 Start sewing the pieces together in the center. Sew up to the top or head hole (see figure 5-2).

6 Sew all the way down to the bottom hole.

7 Stitch back through the center hole. Tie a knot across the very long stitch. If you started on the inside, the knot will be on the inside and you can trim it and make it discreet. If you started on the outside, the knot is on the outside. The knot traps the long stitch, keeping the thread from snagging on anything it might come in contact with (see figure 5-3). Never trim your ends for knots less than ¼ inch (6 mm). It helps to put a tiny dot of adhesive on the top of the knot.

8 Once your signature and explosion page are stitched together, center and adhere them to the fold of the cover.

9 Trim around the edge of the explosion page so that its edges conform to the shape of the cover (see detail photo, below)

Variation
A Book For Rubber Stampers

When designing a book for rubber stampers, I tried to come up with as many places for stamps as possible. This model has three staggered layers of covers. Windows were cut in the back through two layers of covers, and images were printed on both layers, which show through (see detail photo, above). The outermost cover wraps around the two other layers, and its edge is adhered to the inside back cover of the second layer, giving it an asymmetrical look (see figure 5-4). There's only one sheet of text paper nested inside the covers as a signature. The pamphlet stitch is knotted on the inside.

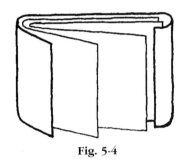

Fig. 5-4

Variation
Altering Page Placement

Folding your pages at varying angles opens up some fun possibilities. This stitch was sewn on a machine, using the longest stitch possible (see detail photos). If you're planning to print on your pages, you'll need to make several imposition models first to make sure that everything appears in its proper place.

BOOK PARTS

Even though artists' books don't always look like ordinary books, they often include traditional book parts. Most artists' and private press books have at least three specific pages: *title page*, *title page verso*, and *colophon*.

TITLE PAGE

The *title page* is usually the first page of a book. It states the title, author, and illustrator of the book, if the author did not do his or her own illustrations. At the bottom of the title page, commercial publishers have to indicate the city and state in which the book was published. As a book artist, you're not required to do this, but it's a good professional habit to get into. A printer's mark often appears above the city and state (see figure SB 5-1).

TITLE PAGE VERSO

The *title page verso* (verso means left hand) is behind the title page. This is where your dedication goes.

It's also a good idea to put copyright information here. Research copyright laws in your country and follow them. Make a copyright statement to protect your work. Under your copyright statement, I recommend listing your address, phone number, fax number, and email address. This allows people who see your book to contact you to buy a copy or invite you to be in an exhibition. Give readers a chance to get in touch.

COLOPHON

The *colophon* is the last page in a private press or artists' book. Everything another artist would be interested in is listed here: the type of paper used, font, information on how the illustrations were created, printing method, information on the book creation process, and names of those who assisted in binding, if any. The colophon ends with the edition size, for example: "This is an edition of 125, of which this copy is number ..."

(then fill in the number for each new copy). The last item on a colophon page is the artist's signature. Always sign your books. If someone is helping you bind or print them, they should sign the books also.

If you choose to have a second edition of your book, mention it in the first edition's colophon. When I did this I said something like "This is a first edition of 1,000. If my binders have courage, there may be a second edition."

If your whole edition is not numbered and signed at the same time, I recommend keeping a scrap of paper listing the last number you used when signing the edition. In a book I read about Roycrofters, a famous private press, the author stated that he questioned the credibility of the press because he had found two books with the same number. I got really careful after that.

Fig. SB 5-1

Two-Signature Pamphlet Stitch Book

*A two-signature pamphlet stitch requires only a single stitch but still looks impressive.
It packs a lot of visual punch for the effort expended: you get twice as many pages
with the same stitch, so it's a great stitch to use when you're making more than one
copy of the same design, such as an edition binding.*

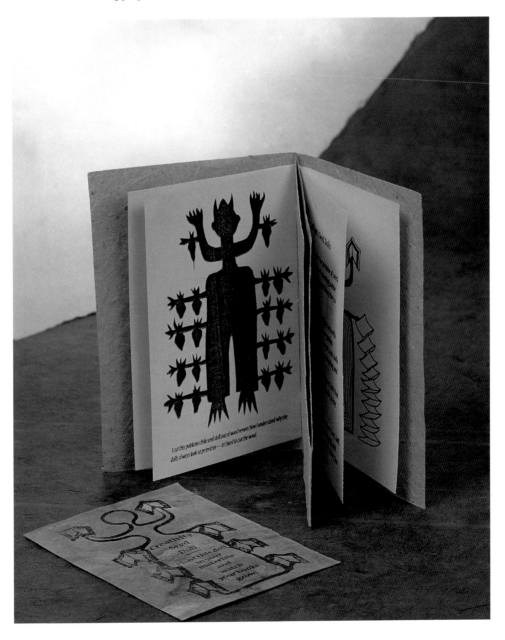

Instructions

1 Create two signatures. In the model, each signature is simply a piece of text weight paper folded in half, but you may add more pages to your signature as you wish.

2 Create a four-panel concertina from cover weight or handmade paper. Pinch the two center panels together to form a pleat (see figures 5-4a and b).

3 Using your hole jig (see instructions on page 69) and sewing cradle (see pages 18-19), poke three holes in the center of each signature. Next, poke corresponding holes in the cover. You'll need two sets of holes. They should be made in the fold on each side of the pleat in the cover.

4 Place a signature on each side of the pleat (see figure 5-5). Sew the structure together with a basic pamphlet stitch (see instructions on page 70 and detail photo, right).

5 In the model, the pleat was oversized, and by applying adhesive to its tail it became a pocket to slip a card or pamphlet into. Trim off the corner of the slipcase. This lets your viewer know there is something inside and makes it easier to retrieve it (see figure 5-6 and detail photo, right). I put a print featuring a seed doll image inside the slipcase. You can also create windows and doors on an enlarged pleat.

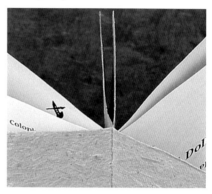

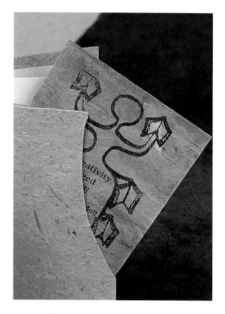

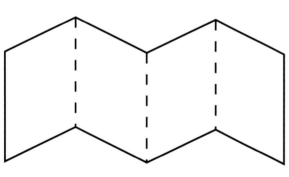

Fig. 5-4a

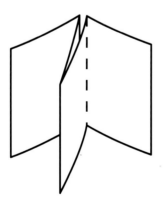

Fig. 5-4b

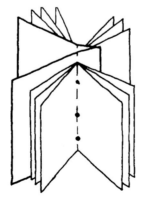

Fig. 5-5

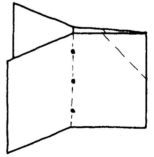

Fig. 5-6

Variation

Two-Signature Pamphlet Stitch with a Tunnel

If you create a large enough center pleat, you can turn it into a tunnel. Just make two more score lines in your pleat, and invert it (see figure 5-6). Because most tunnels use two or more pieces of paper, consider printing an image or text on a separate piece of paper and adhering it inside the tunnel (see figure 5-7 and detail photo, below). Cut a hole the appropriate size for displaying the image or text in your tunnel. You must do this before you stitch up the binding.

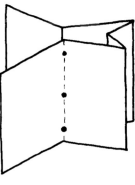

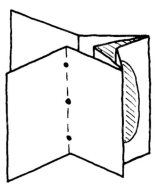

Fig. 5-6

Fig. 5-7

Soft-Cover Journal with a Running Stitch

This binding style is generally used for single-signature books with soft covers. This model has decorative paper strips adhered to the fore edges. It's a simple way to add a lot of personality to a blank journal, and to accent a book's content. A double-layer explosion page pops out from the center fold in this model. Marbled paper strips adhered to the edge of the signature's pages echo the pattern of the marbled explosion page.

Instructions

1 Create your signature by simply folding four pieces of text weight paper in half.

2 For the cover, fold a single piece of cover weight paper in half. The cover is just slightly taller and wider than the signature. Nest your signature in the cover.

3 Using your hole jig (see instructions on page 69) and sewing cradle (see pages 18-19), poke holes through the signature and cover.

4 Start sewing on the inside if you want a discrete knot inside, or on the outside if you plan to attach beads and dangling objects to the thread ends. Starting at either the head or tail, sew in and out the holes all the way along the spine (see figure 5-9).

5 At the end, turn around and sew back down again, in and out the holes (see figure 5-10). Tie a knot when you reach the last hole (see detail photo, below).

6 Create your explosion pages by following the instructions on page 78. In this model, the small explosion page is made from a square of marbled paper and the larger one is made from a square of text weight brown paper.

7 Adhere the marbled square in the center of the larger brown text weight square.

8 Adhere the larger page to the center fold of your book (see detail photo, above).

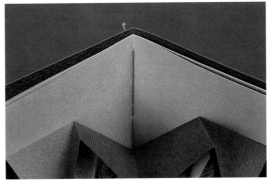

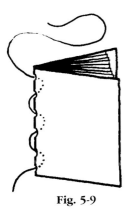

Fig. 5-9

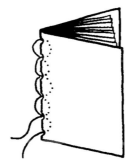

Fig. 5-10

Making an Explosion Page

Explosion pages are a fun touch that can be added any time there are two or more text pages together, or two or more heavy pages together. Here are two different ways to make them:

SIMPLE EXPLOSION PAGE

To make an explosion page or card, start with a square of text weight paper or decorative paper. Fold the square in half diagonally, as a valley fold.

Select two spots along that fold—they must be the same distance in from the edge of the paper.

Fold up, towards the outer edge.

Refold the folds to match the illustration (see figure 5-12a).

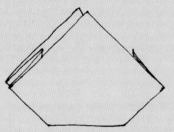

Fig. 5-12a

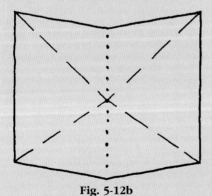

Fig. 5-12b

TRADITIONAL EXPLOSION PAGE

Start with a square of text weight or decorative paper.

Fold it in half, making a mountain fold.

Now fold it in half diagonally twice to create valley folds.

Fold the tips of the paper into the center folds.

Open the paper flat. The fold should be a mountain fold. Now make two diagonal valley folds, corner to corner (see figure 5-12b).

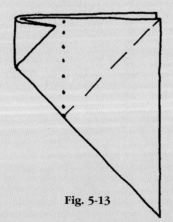

Fig. 5-13

Leave the square folded as a triangle. Take one corner and fold it into the center fold line. Press sharply. Open and invert the corner folds. Repeat this process on all four corners (see figure 5-13).

Adhere the two sides that aren't folded onto your page. The center point of the explosion paper must be flush with the signature's spine or the text pages won't open completely.

Variation
Using Creative Explosion Pages

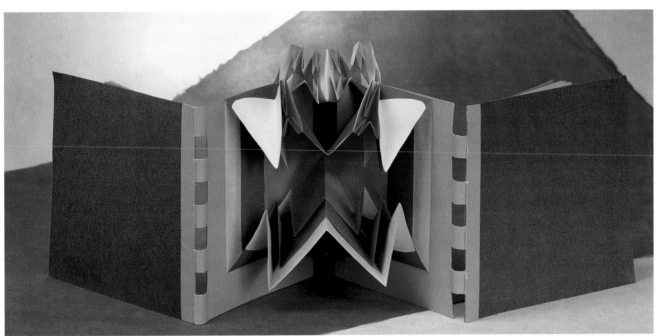

Although it appears to be a simple four-panel concertina, this model reveals a delightful surprise. My binding assistant Tracy Aplin shaped a dragon's head out of explosion pages, complete with a flaming throat, flaming nostrils, and luminescent green eyes, and bound it into the book's center fold. Two pamphlets are stitched into its folds.

The explosion pages are concealed in a fold that's held closed by a skewer (for more on using skewers in bindings, see Recessed Skewer Binding, pages 111-124). Combining different binding styles opens up new opportunities to add secrets and surprises to a book.

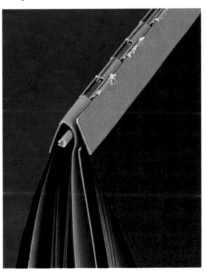

Gallery

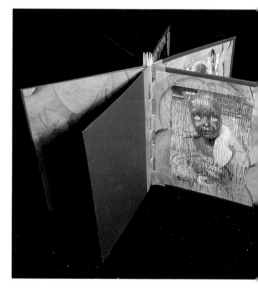

Above: Martha Hall, *Tattoo*, 1998. 4⅝ x 4⅝ inches (11.74 x 11.74 cm). Dos à dos pamphlet stitch, closed; paste, board, pastel and rice papers, lokta; rubber stamped and laser printed. Photo by Jay York

Center left: Genie Shenk, *Piano Dreams*, 1998. 4½ x 15 x 15 inches (11.4 x 38.1 x 38.1 cm). Single-signature books; wood, paper, mica and found object; photocopied and laser printed.

Center right: R.H. Starr, Jr., *Daddy Loves Me Version 4*, 1994. 8½ x 7 x ¾ inches (21.6 x 17.8 x 1.9 cm). Piano hinge binding, closed; paste paper; photographs; skewers.

Left: Diane Cassidy, *Diane Cassidy in Turkiye*, 1996. 6½ x 10 inches (16.5 x 25.4 cm). Concertina; board, card stock, digital-collage photos, service bureau output.

Tacket Binding

Tacket binding, or tacketing, is an ancient technique, probably dating from the second century A.D. At the Nag Hammadi excavation in Egypt, archaeologists found 10 tacketed books. These books date from the third and fourth centuries A.D. and are the oldest intact bound books found in the world to date.

Tacket binding is usually done on a single-signature structure. The ones found at Nag Hammadi had between 132 and 148 pieces of parchment (goatskin or sheepskin) folded in half and nested together into signatures. That's bulky! Bookbinders today try to keep signatures down to four pieces of paper or parchment.

Tacket binding requires pairs of holes for sewing. The stitching is a focal point on the spine, so your pairs of holes should be evenly placed. The best way to get evenly placed holes is to create a hole jig (refer to page 69) and a sewing cradle (see pages 18-19). You'll need both for all the books in the chapter.

There are quite a few variations within tacket binding, including several multi-signature techniques. We'll cover a few of the options. In tacket binding, the thread shows; it's an exposed binding. This means all the holes in each signature's spine, and on ribbons, tapes, and covers, have to line up. Tape refers to a flat, ribbon-like strip, made of either real ribbon, leather, or any sturdy, flexible paper, such as lokta. If paper is used, it should be folded in half or thirds lengthwise for extra strength.

Go to your local knitting or weaving store and see what kind of cotton or linen threads they stock. Look for thick thread or thin cord; either type is suitable. Hemp cord is my preference for tacketing.

Originally, tacket binding was made with thread-thin pieces of goatskin parchment. Skins have a natural adhesive that is activated with water. Short pieces of thread-thin goatskin were cut, and their ends were dipped in water. The pieces would then be sewn through a signature and cover, and the ends would be wrapped together and remain in place. Since we use yarn or cord these days, we stick the ends together with PVA.

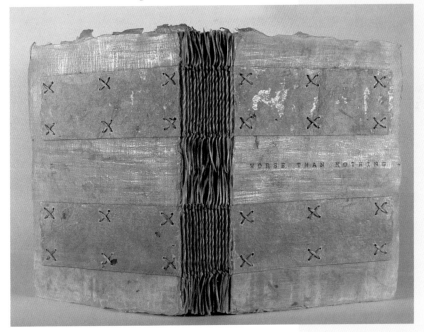

Jody Alexander, *Worse Than Nothing*, 1999.
7 x 5 inches (17.8 x 12.7 cm). Tacketed binding;
Kozo and gampi papers, photocopy transfers.

Dos à Dos Single and Double-Signature Tacket Binding

This model is a book about the historic ego battle between Pharaoh Ptolemy V and King Eumenes II, each of whom developed his library as a status symbol. The pharaoh's library was in Alexandria, Egypt, and the king's library was at Pergamum, near modern-day Bergama, Turkey. The two men's rivalry resulted both in the development of parchment for use in books, and the codex format—the book as we know it today.

Assuming not everyone knew where Pergamum was, I drew a map of the eastern end of the Mediterranean Sea for the inside of the book. The map is larger than the inside of the front cover, so I created a flap that folds back, and I "tipped in" the map.

Materials

1 piece of printmaking paper (for the cover), 5¾ x 13¼ inches (14.6 x 33.65 cm)

1 piece of cream-colored text weight paper (for the map), 5½ x 6½ inches (14 x 16.5 cm)

3 pieces of beige text weight paper, 5½ x 8½ inches (14 x 21.6 cm)

6 pieces of cream-colored text weight paper, 5½ x 8¼ inches (14 x 20.95 cm)

1 piece of printmaking paper (for the wrapper),12½ x 3¾ inches (31.8 x 9.52 cm)

Note: To tip in an illustration, lay a bead of adhesive on one edge of your page and adhere your illustration in place. Tipping in, instead of applying adhesive to the entire surface, creates much less moisture, less buckling, and fewer placement problems.

Fig. 6-1

Fig. 6-2

Instructions

1 Fold each of your six cream-colored signature pages in half individually (folding as a group telescopes the edges; that means that they don't line up at both fore edges, only on one side). Nest two folded cream-colored pages together inside a folded beige signature wrapper (see figure 6-1). Create two more signatures in the same way.

2 Your cover is a three-panel Z fold concertina made with the printmaking cover paper (see dos à dos format on page 34, and detail photo, page 84). You'll be sewing one signature into one of the folds, and two signatures into the other. Create a mark at 4 ⅜ inches (11.11 cm) in from both ends for the folds. Because the double-signature side requires a narrow spine, add another mark at ⅛ inch (3 mm) further in. Pressure score and fold at all your marks. The ⅛ inch (3 mm) space becomes the spine for the double-signature side, creating enough room to accommodate both signatures (see figure 6-2).

3 You'll need your sewing cradle and a hole jig for the next step. The height of your hole jig should accurately match the height of your cover. For the single-signature side of the book, place one signature in your sewing cradle. Create marks on your hole jig where you want the pairs of holes to be. In the model they're at 1 inch (2.5 cm) and 2¼ inches (5.08 cm) in from both the head and the tail (see figure 6-3).

4 Lay the hole jig inside the signature, line up the signature's head and tail with the marks on the hole jig, and poke holes in the signature's spine according to the marks (see figure 6-4). Repeat the process for the single-signature side of the cover; place the single fold of the cover in the joint of the sewing cradle, place the hole jig on top of it, and poke the holes.

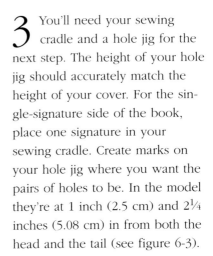

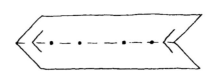

Fig. 6-3

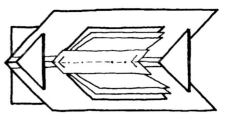

Fig. 6-4

5 For the double-signature side of the book, each signature fits into one of the two folds on either side of the spine you created in step 2. One at a time, place each of the cover's two folds in the joint of the sewing cradle, together with a signature. Place the hole jig on top, make your marks, and poke holes.

6 Starting from the outside, sew into one hole and out its partner hole. Leave enough thread free at the ends so you can twist them together (see figure 6-5). I used cotton crochet thread for

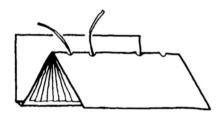

Fig. 6-5

Fig. 6-6

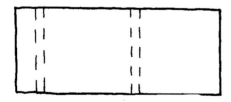

Fig. 6-7

this model. Since the thread was thin, I doubled it to give it visual weight.

7 Now start tacketing. Twist your thread ends around each other (see figure 6-6). After twisting them together, run a thin bead of PVA or fast-setting adhesive on top of the twist. Hold it for 30 seconds, then sew the other set of holes (repeat for as many

pairs of holes as you have created). Repeat this process for both signatures on the double-signature spine (see detail photos, center and below).

8 After your adhesive is dry, trim the thread ends or add beads and other dangling objects if you like. There are lots of opportunities here.

Whenever possible, make a wrapper, cuff, slipcase, or box for a book (see detail photo, right, page 85). This is especially important for books you've taken the trouble to research and illustrate. The cuff for this model was Gocco printed on each side, one with hieroglyphics and the other with ancient Greek text. The height and depth of the

book—5¾ x ¼ inches (12.7 cm x 6 mm)—were measured, scored, and folded on printmaking paper to create the cuff (see figure 6-7). These measurements were repeated to create the backside of the cuff, leaving a ½-inch (1.3 cm) flap to adhere in place on one side. Allow for a little leeway in your cuff's size. You need enough space to let it slip on and off easily, but not too much or it will fall off.

COMMONPLACE BOOKS

Commonplace books are collections of quotations. In the 18th and 19th centuries, it was considered proper for European or American gentlemen (and some women) to create a commonplace book and have it printed and beautifully bound. The creator would then give copies of it to various libraries, establishing his or her identity for posterity. I don't see how one person's quotes are relevant to another's philosophy, but I do recommend starting a commonplace book for yourself.

Quotes are frequently needed when making artists' books. If you're lacking inspiration for text, quotes can be an easy way out of writing original material. Having a few favorites available saves the time and frustration of searching for the perfect quote. You may choose to focus on a theme, picking favorite quotes by an individual or favorite lines from movies or songs. There are lots of options. Be observant of copyright laws.

This collaborative commonplace book was a fundraiser for my local book arts guild. Collaborative books have a life and spontaneity that's impossible to re-create by yourself. We had such fun with it, and the result is a very vibrant book.

North Redwoods Book Arts Guild, *Commonplace Collaborative Book*, 1995. 7¼ x 5¾ inches (18.09 x 14.60 cm). Concertina; board, various papers; various printing techniques.

Multisignature Tacket Binding

In this model, the signature wrappers are die-cut folders, but you can create the signature wrapper or cover of your choice. An extra-long piece of paper is fine. Historically, multisignature tacket bindings were done with chunks of leather. I'm substituting four-ply museum board for it here.

Die-cutting is the process of cutting paper into shapes. A variety of pre-cut dies are available, or you can custom order them. Check at your local rubber stamp stores to see if they carry them. You might also ask about them at the educational resource center for your school district, or a large elementary school. Schools use these dies for bulletin board cutouts in classrooms.

Instructions

1 Create signatures and signature wrappers in the style of your choice. In the model, there are nine signature wrappers. Signatures are nested inside six of them, each with four sheets of text weight paper, folded in half. The remaining three wrappers don't have signatures; they're decorated with artists' stamps and faux postage.

2 Using your hole jig and sewing cradle, create two sets of two holes each in your wrappers. Create corresponding holes in your signatures. Nest each of your signatures in cover wrappers.

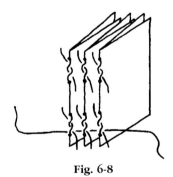

Fig. 6-8

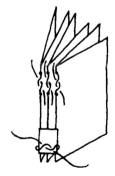

Fig. 6-9

3 Follow the instructions for tacket binding in steps 6 and 7 on page 84. Tacket one set of holes in each wrapper (and signature when applicable), and then the other. All of your holes and tacketing must line up. This model uses hemp cord.

4 Hold all your signature wrappers together and measure their total thickness. The width of the book's spine will be equal to this measurement. Measure the space between two holes in your sets of holes (the space should be equal in both sets, so you only need to do this measurement on one of them).

5 Cut two small pieces of four-ply museum board to match the measurements you just took. Each piece of board should be as wide as the book's spine, and a little longer than the space between two holes in a set.

6 Stack your signatures on top of each other. Line up all the tacketing.

7 Cut a new piece of thread, at least 1 inch (2.5 cm) longer than twice the width of the book. Starting with one end of one set of holes, sew under the tacketing in all of the signatures (see figure 6-8).

8 Wrap the ends of your thread around your piece of board, twist them together, and add adhesive, making a tacket (see figure 6-9). You will need to cut a small groove into the board to hold the tacket in place (see detail photo, below).

9 Repeat steps 7 and 8 for the other end of the set of holes, and the other edge of the piece of board.

10 Repeat steps 7 through 9 for the other set of holes.

Finish your book by adding artists' stamps or other decorative images inside the wrappers.

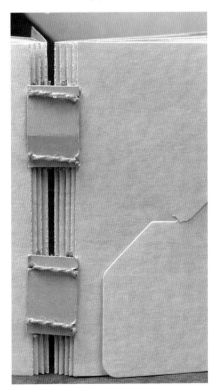

Variation
Staggered Holes

In this model, there are seven signatures. Each has two holes instead of four, and the holes are staggered, meaning they're in a different location in each signature. The holes in the center signature are closer together than in all the others.

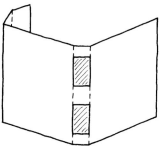

Fig. 6-10

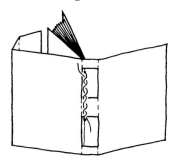

Fig. 6-11

Fig. 6-12

Create your signatures, each with a wrapper; the signature wrappers in the model have different colors, alternating from cream to bronze and back again. This adds visual depth.

The book's cover is made from a single piece of paper which wraps around the front and back of the book. Your cover paper should be the height and double the width of a signature, plus the depth of all the signatures stacked together for the spine. Take the piece of cover paper and score and fold your front cover, spine, back cover, and fore edge spine (which will be the same depth as the other spine).

This model has also has closure flap that is scored and folded from the fore edge spine, and wraps around the front cover.

To display the binding, cut holes in the spine, leaving a band at the head and tail to hold the cover together, and in the center to tacket over (see figure 6-10).

Starting with your first signature, tacket through the two holes and

across the cover's center band (see figure 6-11).

For the second signature, start tacketing at the hole in the tail end. Again, tacket through both the holes and across the cover's center band. Repeat until all the signatures are bound onto the cover. Notice that the holes in each signature are staggered (see figure 6-12). Trim your ends.

Soft Spine Book with Multisignature Tacketing

In this variation, tapes made from strips of paper take the place of the pieces of heavy board on the spine. The paper tapes are adhered to the covers at the head and tail of the spine. Soft spine bindings work especially well for artists' books because of their display value. They're great for showcasing illustrations, calligraphy, or text.

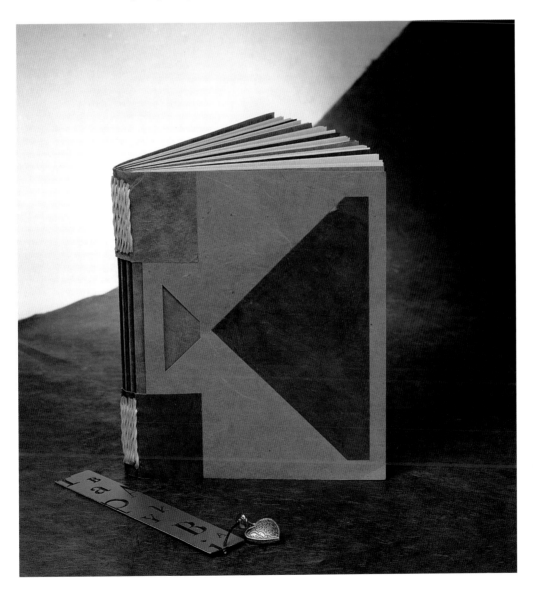

Instructions

1 Create your signatures. In the model, there are six, each made up of four pieces of text weight paper, folded, and nested inside a piece of brown cover weight paper.

2 Stack your signatures together to measure their total thickness.

3 Create a cover from a single piece of cover weight paper. It will be the same height as your signatures and its length will be equal to twice the width of your signatures, plus the thickness of signatures stacked together. Score and fold a spine on the cover paper.

4 Cut a hole in the spine (this will expose the signatures). Instead of leaving a band in the center of the spine (see figure 6-10 on page 88), leave bands only at the head and tail of the spine, and extend the hole onto the front and back covers. In the model, geometric shapes were also cut into the front and back covers (see detail photo, left).

5 Cut two pieces of sturdy paper to use as tapes. Since you'll be poking holes in the paper, it needs to be strong or reinforced paper so that the holes you poke don't enlarge, form a tear, and disbind your book. The length and width of the tapes varies depending on the size of your book—they should be long enough to wrap around the spine of the book and attach to the front and back covers, and wide enough to cover the bands that you created in step 4 at the head and tail of the spine.

6 Adhere your tapes to the covers, flush with the head and tail (see detail photo, bottom right).

7 Using your hole jig and sewing cradle, mark and poke two sets of two holes each in the signatures, signature wrappers, and the cover (the holes will go through the cover and the strong paper tapes).

8 Choose your thread. Tacket the signatures (see instructions on page 84) directly onto the cover and through the tapes at both the head and tail (see figure 6-13).

9 Use leftover thread or cord to cover the tacketing. Simply cut it to an appropriate size and adhere it to the tapes over the tacketing (see detail photo, below).

10 For interest, brown cover weight paper was cut into triangles and adhered to the covers. The shape echoes the small cutout on the front and back covers, and the color complements the varying shades used in the signatures, cover, and tapes.

Fig. 6-13

Variation

Substituting Concertina for Tapes

This model is made in the same manner as the previous project except each of the tapes has an eight-panel concertina folded into the portion that stretches over the book's spine. Holes are poked in the mountain folds of the concertinas, and each signature is tacketed into a mountain fold. This style allows the holes to spread out, so they don't tear. This binding allows the pages to spread out, so it's also a great style for display (see figure 6-14 and detail photo, below).

In this model, leftover pieces of hemp cord are adhered to the cover of the book in a decorative pattern (see detail photo, below).

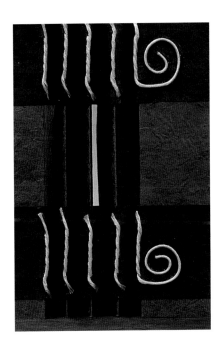

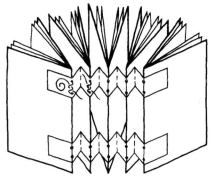

Fig. 6-14

THE DRESSED BOOK

These books have been very popular at my workshops. Their structure is simple; just a few pieces of long, skinny text paper with something pretty wrapped around them to resemble a coat or garment. The stitch is not tacket binding, just two holes and a stitch. Instead of twisting the thread as you do in tacketing, knots are usually tied on top of the book.

To create a simple dressed book, poke two holes at the top of a signature, sew through them and tie a knot (see figure SB 6-1). Decide what you will use as a stole (a kind of wrap). My model's stole also has a long panel, so it acts as a slipcase (see figure SB 6-2).

If you taper a piece of text paper, you can create a poncho as a wrapper. One model features two different lengths of text paper, and a stole on top (see photo, above). Finally, I gave one book a coat instead of a stole. There are no rules, so there are no limits.

If you like, add an arm to your wrapper. Just cut regular text paper into an L shape. One of my models has a sash (see figure SB 6-3).

I designed one book with tall skinny pages, then finished it with a folded crossbar to add arms to the wrapper (see SB 6-4). Finally, I created a slipcase in the form of a jacket to complete it.

My kimono book is the only dressed book that is different. It's bound on the sides. Each layer overlaps in the front, with a slightly deeper cut for the neckline. A simple "obi cuff" holds the book together.

Shereen LaPlantz, *Dressed Books*, Various decorative and oriental papers.

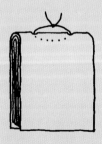

Fig. SB 6-1

Fig. SB 6-2

Fig. SB 6-3

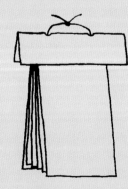

Fig. SB 6-4

Long Stitch as Multisignature Binding

This model features a variation on the multisignature tacket binding style seen on page 90. It uses the long stitch. The long stitch is like half a running stitch. It doesn't turn around and come back up or down a spine, though. Instead, it's tied at both ends.

Instructions

1 First, prepare your signatures. In the model there are nine, each made up four pieces of text weight paper in alternating colors, folded in half. These signatures aren't wrapped.

2 Create your covers from a heavy cover weight paper. The front cover will be the height and width of your signatures. Simply start with a piece of paper twice the width of your signatures, then score, and fold it in half.

3 The back cover is the height and width of the signatures, plus a 2-inch (5.1 cm) stub inside the back cover, plus a spine on the fore edge, and a flap equal to just over half the width of your cover (see figure 6-15). On one end of the back cover paper, score and fold the stub. Next, stack your signatures together and measure their total thickness. This measurement will equal the depth of the fore edge spine. Score and fold the spine and the flap on the other end of your paper.

4 Using a hole jig and a sewing cradle, poke three sets of two holes each in each signature.

5 Sew in and out of your holes, starting and ending on the inside. Rather than twist your ends together, like the style on page 84, tie a knot at both the head and tail end holes (see figure 6-16). Repeat for each signature.

6 Again, measure the thickness of your signatures stacked together. Measure the distance between the two holes in your sets of holes. Cut three pieces of board to match these measurements (the boards should be slightly longer than the space between two holes in a set).

7 Starting with the front cover, tacket the covers and signatures to the boards using the process described on in steps 7 and 8 page 87 (see detail photo, right).

8 Pull the back flap around the front to close the covers (see detail photo, below).

You may want to add decorative papers on the inside of the covers of your book for interest. Simply cut a square or whatever shape your model requires, center it in the middle of your cover panel, and adhere it to the inside of the cover.

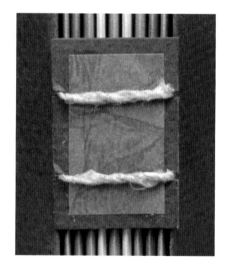

Fig. 6-15

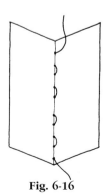

Fig. 6-16

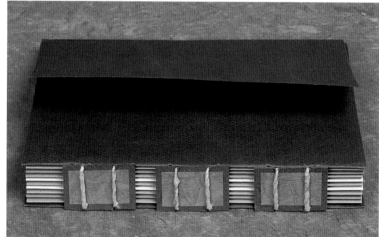

Gallery

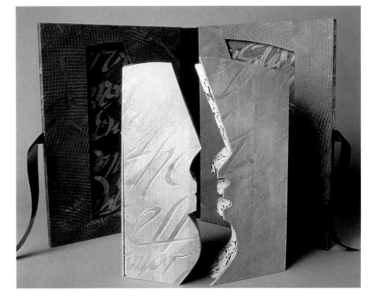

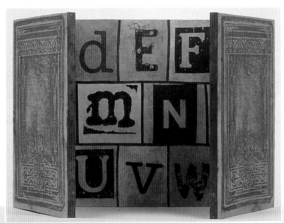

Top: Joan M. Soppe, *About the Linens*, 1995. 5½ x 4 x 2 inches (14 x 10.2 x 5.1 cm). Dos à dos Coptic stitch; mixed media; letterpress.

Center: Viviana Lombrozo, *Conversation*, 1998. 10 x 9 x 6 inches (25.4 x 22.9 x 15.2 cm). Coptic binding; paste and papers; calligraphy. Photo by Howard Lippin

Bottom left: Peter Madden, *P's and Q's*, 1999. 8 x 13 inches (20.3 x 33 cm). Wooden-hinged triptych, closed; mixed media.

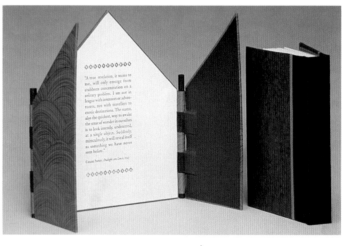

Top: Emily Martin, *So On and So On*, 1995. 2½ x 2¼ x 1¾ inches (6.4 x 5.71 x 4.45 cm). Dos à dos Coptic stitch; printmaking paper; photocopied. Photo by Meryl Marek

Center left: Debra Madison, *Traditional Hand Bookbinding/The Artist and the Book*, 1999. 6 inches x 4 feet (15.2 cm x 1.21 m). Dos à dos concertina, open; mixed media; photocopied and gold stamped.

Center right: Mitzi Lindgren, *Altar Book and Flat Case Binding*, 1997. 6½ x 7 inches (16.5 x 17.8 cm). Case bound piano hinge triptych; paste and pastel papers; letterpress and blind embossing.

Left: Catherine Michaelis, *Flower*, 1996. 3 x 5 inches (7.6 x 12.7 cm). Cloth-hinged, double-sided panel binding; decorative, Oriental and printmaking papers, fabric, board; letterpress. Photo by Kim Newall

Coptic Stitch

The Coptic stitch came to us from the Copts, a religious group that originated as an early Christian sect in Egypt and northern Africa. Early Coptic books had a major influence on the bookbinding structures of many cultures throughout history. The Moors in North Africa absorbed Coptic binding styles into their own Islamic binding patterns. Later, during the time of Roman Empire, Coptic bindings spread throughout the region surrounding the Mediterranean sea. All Western European medieval bindings show a Coptic influence.

The Coptic stitch is a distinctive part of Coptic books. All Coptic stitch books I have seen, and the one that I own, have three lines of stitching. Everything the Copts do is symbolic of their faith, and I can only surmise that these three lines represent the Holy Trinity.

Today, all variations of Coptic stitch can be made with either a single needle or double needles, and with a hard or soft cover. Double-needle Coptic stitch books with soft covers seem to be the easiest to make. Because the spine is exposed in all Coptic stitch bindings, these books open beautifully and easily, displaying the text and illustrations.

If your first Coptic stitch book looks unprofessional, don't panic. It's probably a tension problem. With practice the problem should smooth out.

Helen Petre, *Condo of Cards*, 1999. 6 x 7¼ x ¾ inches (15.2 x 18.4 x 1.9 cm). Origami folds and pamphlet stitch; printmaking paper and card deck; acrylic paint in monoprinting. Photo by Donald R. Weeke

Stub Book: Simple Coptic Stitch (Double Needles and a Soft Cover)

The Coptic stitch can be used for many different types of binding—this is only one example. A book with this type of binding is called a stub book because of the style of its signatures. Each page and signature wrapper has a small stub (similar to a tab) folded onto one end.

STUB BOOK: SIMPLE COPTIC STITCH

Stub binding is used primarily for three reasons:

1) When you add something extra to your pages, like a tunnel, collage, or embossing, the fore edge of your book tends to flair open. Adding stubs, even just 2-inch-wide (5.1 cm) pieces of paper to your signatures compensates for the extra fore edge bulk.

2) They're useful when you want to tip in an illustration.

3) They're good for books made with short papers because the paper doesn't have to be folded in half for binding.

Coptic stitch automatically fattens up the spine of a book, so it's a perfect binding for bulky fore edges.

In this model, each of the text weight signature pages was preprinted with clip art, and a clip art image was adhered onto the cover.

Materials

22 pieces of white text paper, 4 x 7¼ inches (10.2 x 18.4 cm)

4 pieces of red pastel paper, 4 x 7¼ inches (10.2 x 18.4 cm)

2 pieces of red pastel paper, 4 x 6¼ inches (10.2 x 15.8 cm)

10 pieces of blue pastel paper, 4 x 7¼ inches (10.2 x 18.4 cm)

1 length of waxed linen, 65 inches (1.65 m)

2 blunt-ended needles, sized to fit your thread choice

Note: Waxed linen is especially nice for this stitch. The wax holds each stitch in place, creating better tension. It also comes in many colors. Look for waxed linen in weaving and basketry supply stores. Because the thread is a bit thicker, the blunt-ended needles have to be a bit larger. Keep them as small as possible (a big needle means a big hole). Both of your needles have to be the same size. Don't use curved needles because they're sharp, and can poke new holes or create gouges in your signatures.

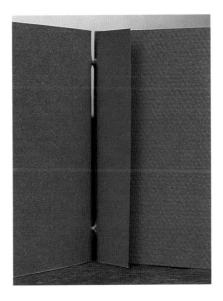

Instructions
Creating the Signatures

1 Measure, score, and fold 1 inch (2.5 cm) in on one side of all of your pieces of pastel paper except the two shorter pieces of red paper. The short flap created by this fold is your stub (see detail photo center, below).

2 The short and long pieces of red paper have the same dimensions after the stub has been folded on the longer pieces. Each short piece will adhere to each longer piece as a reinforcement so these pieces can serve as covers. Line up each short red piece flush with the fore edge of each longer red piece, apply adhesive, and join them together (the stub will extend from the longer piece, beyond the part that is now reinforced). These pieces are now your front and back covers. Set them aside.

3 Fold a 1 inch (2.5 cm) stub on each piece of text weight paper.

4 Alternating the stubs from front to back, nest the text paper into five signatures with four pieces of paper each.

5 Nest each signature inside two blue pieces of paper, which will serve as signature wrappers (see figure 7-1). The stubs on the blue signature wrappers will alternate too (see detail photo, above).

6 Create a one-page signature with a piece of white text weight paper. Nest it inside a red piece of paper with a stub, and nest both pieces inside one of the red covers (see detail photo, below).

7 Repeat step 6 for another one-page signature, and nest it in the other red cover.

For the Binding

8 Create a hole jig with two holes. Measure in from the head and tail, and mark where each hole will be on your hole jig (they should be equally spaced in from the head and tail). The stitch lines are the focal point of the spine, so correct measurements are important. Poke holes in all your signatures, including the front cover and back cover signatures, which are wrapped in the front and back covers.

9 To figure out how much thread you need, measure from head to tail, multiply that number by the number of signatures, then double it (because you're using double needles), and add a little extra for a comfort zone. A comfort zone accommodates the thread going through the needles and tying knots. If your thread is too short, it's uncomfortable to work with.

10 Thread one end of the linen thread through each needle, leaving short tails. Starting on the inside of the front cover signature, sew through one hole with one needle, and through the other hole with the other needle. Even up the lengths, and place the cover in the middle.

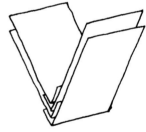

Fig. 7-1

Fig. 7-2

11 To add on the first signature with a blue wrapper, lay it next to the front cover signature. Using one needle, sew into one of its holes (it doesn't matter if you start with head or tail). Sew out the next hole—it's the only other hole in the signature. Using the other needle and thread, start sewing the other hole (see figure 7-2). There should be two threads in each hole now, one going in and one coming out (see figure 7-3). Snug everything up, making a smooth, even tension, rather than a tight tension.

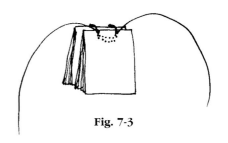

Fig. 7-3

BOTANICAL BOOKS

Botanical books feature outstanding illustrations of plants or flowers. Although we have examples of botanical books dating back centuries, their popularity reached its height in the 17th and 18th centuries. Traveling expeditions collected every specimen of flora and fauna they encountered to show off to the academic community back in Europe. Groups often had a staff artist to recreate the collected samples in beautiful watercolors and line drawings which were bound in books. Botanical books are some of the most sumptuous books I've seen. The illustrations are often on oversize pages that fold out. Although we may have different motives for making them, these books are still very popular today.

If you want to make your own botanical book, you can use available clip art or rubber stamps, take photos, or draw illustrations yourself. Think of a theme. If you decide to do a book on bamboo, will a panda be peeking out from behind the bamboo? If you prefer roses, will you display tea roses? Will this be a gardening book or a plant lore book? Will you include just the name of the plant with the illustration or more?

Carla Tenret, *Iris*, 2000. 9 x 11¾ inches (22.9 x 29.84 cm). Calligraphy with technical pen, italic variation; drawing paper.

You may want to form the text as a calligram (the text written in a shape, such as a flower). For example, if you had a poem about an iris, the text would fit on the petals of the iris illustration (see below). As a jumping off point, you may want to use the Victorian "language of flowers." Kate Greenaway's book on the subject (Dover, 1993) describes the symbolic meaning of hundreds of types of flowers. You could use flowers to spell out a message (with a key to the code included, of course). There are great possibilities.

I recommend taking a look at the *Mira Calligraphiae Monumenta* (J. Paul Getty Museum, 1992), an outstanding calligraphy specimen book with gorgeous botanical illustrations. The calligraphy is wonderful, but the botanical illustrations are breathtaking. I've never seen better. Don't try to match the Mira. Just have fun.

TIP
SEW FROM THE MIDDLE OUT-
WARD. IT'S EASIER TO FISH THE
NEEDLES OUT THAT WAY.

12 Add on the another signature with a blue wrapper. Repeat the process described in steps 10 and 11. After both threads have been sewn through the new signature, start the chain stitch of the Coptic stitch by following the instructions below.

13 Using one needle at a time, skip the last stitch you created (the stitch between the first and second blue wrapper signatures), and sew under the previous stitch (the stitch between the front cover signature and the first signature with the blue wrapper), creating a link stitch. Do this with both threads and needles (see figures 7-4 and 7-5). Snug up the tension. Smooth, consistent tension is important, not tight tension. You need to leave a loop for the chain of this stitch.

14 Repeat steps 12 and 13. Add on a new signature

and sew through it. Sew under the stitch before the last stitch you created. Snug up the tension. Repeat this process until all the signatures are sewn together.

15 The last stitch is the same as all the others, except there's no new signature to sew into. When you're finished stitching the Coptic stitch, sew into the back cover signature with both needles. Open up the cover, find the two ends, and tie a knot. Trim the ends (see figure 7-6 and detail photo, below).

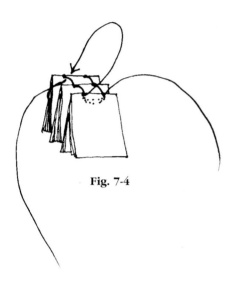

Fig. 7-4

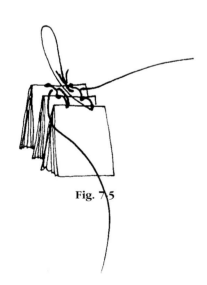

Fig. 7-5

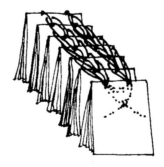

Fig. 7-6

Variation
Individually-Wrapped Signatures with Coptic Stitch

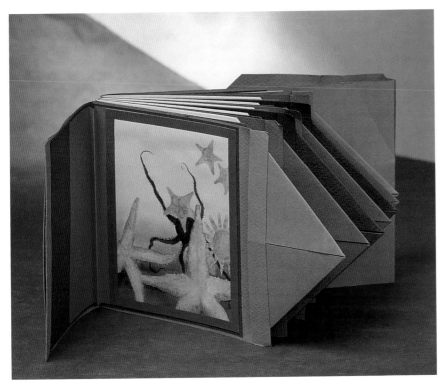

The inspiration for this model came from Japanese gift wrapping. It features a type of fold designed to wrap money. This wrapper style can also be used for a single-signature pamphlet stitch binding or in almost any other style of binding.

Each of the signatures is made up of four pieces of text weight paper folded in half. The corners are cut from the edge of the pages for interest.

Each signature has a wrapper made from a piece of pastel paper, 5 x 12½ inches (12.7 x 31.8), but

you can adjust your sizes and use any paper that folds easily.

To make each wrapper, take your paper and fold back one end to half the width of the strip, plus ½ inch (1.3 cm) more. The fold for this model was at 3 inches (7.6 cm). Mark the center of your fold (see figure 7-8).

Fold both ends of inward, stopping at the center mark (see figure 7-9). You'll have a tab remaining at the end of the fold. Fold it over the two flaps you just created. Apply adhesive to the tab to keep it in place. Otherwise it will come open with extensive use.

Trim the other corners of the other side of your long piece of paper. Fold the paper almost in half. To close the wrapper, you'll tuck the end with trimmed corners into the point you created (see figure 7-10), but first you'll need to sew the signature into the wrapper, so set this piece aside for now.

Fig. 7-8

Fig. 7-9

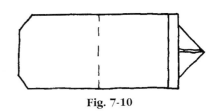

Fig. 7-10

Next, create your covers. For the front cover, one end of paper has a point, made in the same manner as the signature wrapper's point. Rather than trim the corners of the other end of the paper (as you do with the signature wrapper), fold that end into a point as well, apply adhesive, and attach the point to the cover. You'll have an

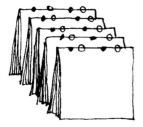

Fig. 7-10a

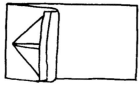

Fig. 7-11

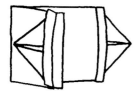

Fig. 7-12

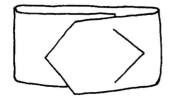

Fig. 7-13

open pocket under the point (see figures 7-11 and 7-12).

For the back cover, you'll need an piece of paper that's long enough to wrap around the front of the book. On one end of the paper, cut a point, and cut a flap into the point (see figure 7-13). The point on the front of the book will fit into this flap when the book is closed, so measure it carefully. Score and fold indentations on the paper near the base of this flap, so that the cover will fit snugly around the signature wrappers. Create a point on the other end of the back cover paper.

Poke four holes in the signatures, wrappers, and covers. The spacing of the holes in this model is unusual—there are single holes near the head and tail and a set of holes near the center (see figure 7-10a).

Wrap your signatures.

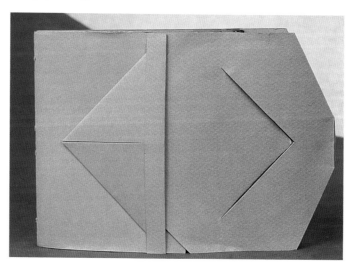

To bind the signatures and covers, use two pairs of stitches or chain lines. Rather than use four needles at once, use two needles to make the first pair of stitch lines. Starting with your front cover, follow the instructions for double-needle Coptic stitch steps 8 through 13 for the Stub

Book. The lines overlap inside the signatures, and are different colors, for visual interest. Continue to add signatures until you get to the back cover (see detail photo, above).

Finally, wrap the elongated back cover around to the front, and insert it into the open pocket on the front (see detail photo, left).

Single-Needle Coptic Stitch with a Hard Cover

There are many more traditional and historical variations of Coptic stitch. Here are some examples. Feel free to develop your own, too.

Refer to the Techniques section on page 20 for information on punching holes in board for covers.

Instructions

1 Prepare your signatures. The model uses two pieces of text weight paper in the center of each signature, wrapped in three different types of paper (one piece of each).

2 Using a hole jig as a guide, poke five evenly-spaced holes in the signatures.

3 Cut two pieces of board (any heavy noncorrugated board will do) the size of your signatures. This is an exposed-spine binding, so your covers have to be flush with the head and tail of your signatures, allowing you to display pages when the book is open.

4 Cut two pieces of covering paper, approximately 2 inches (5.1 cm) larger than the boards in height and width.

5 Cut two pieces of endpaper about 1 inch (2.5 cm) shorter than the boards in height and width. If your endpapers are sheer and your board can be seen

through them, adhere an opaque piece of paper (the same size) under them first. If your covering paper is thick, consider adhering your endpaper to a cut piece of file folder or 10-point stock paper. This hides the difference in thickness, and the inside cover looks neat and professional.

6 Apply adhesive to your covering paper, then center your board.

7 Since a mitered corner has been shown (see figure 4-17 on page 65), use a universal corner. This type of corner is created by folding in the tip of a corner and making a square on the board (see figure 7-14). Repeat on all four corners. This corner style is good for fabrics, thin papers, and generally any covering material.

8 Attach the corners you just made by folding over the edges, and pressing them in place. Repeat on all four sides.

9 Repeat the whole process for the second board. This method will give the appearance of a mitered corner with a slightly blunt tip (see figure 7-15).

10 Poke holes in the covers to correspond with the holes in the signatures. They should be approximately 1/4 inch (6 mm) in from the spine edge.

11 After all your holes are poked and drilled, measure your thread using the following formula: measure the height of the book by the number of signatures, plus two for the covers, and add a comfort zone. Do not double the length; this is a single-needle stitch.

12 Thread your needle and start on the inside of the first signature. Sew out of the first hole. Sew into the first hole in the cover. Sew around it twice, continually adjusting the cover's position so that its edge is even with

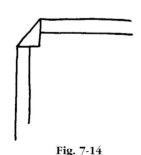

Fig. 7-14

Fig. 7-15

Fig. 7-16

the signature's spine. Work until you think it's perfect. Snug up the tension (see figure 7-16).

13 Sew back into the first hole of the signature. Tie a knot with the loose end. Tip: Don't trim the ends yet. The long thread may get trimmed by mistake. There's time to trim when the binding is finished.

14 Sew into the next hole in the signature. Repeat the process of sewing twice through the cover and back into the signature, and snug up the tension.

15 Continue until the sewing is finished at the last hole in the cover. Rather than return to the first signature, add in a new one and sew into the corresponding hole for that signature (see figure 7-17).

16 Sew up through the next hole in the signature and start the link or chain part of the Coptic stitch. Skip the stitch

between the cover and second signatures, and sew under the stitch between the cover and first signature (see figure 7-18).

17 Continue until all the holes are sewn. At the end of a signature, add a new signature, and continue sewing, repeating the process. Continually snug up the tension. Smooth and even is the desired tension (see detail photo, top right).

18 To add the back cover, sew it on just like the front cover. Lay it next to the last signature, and sew through the corresponding hole twice. Rather than sewing back into the signature, do the link or chain part of the Coptic stitch. Sew under not your last stitch, but the one before it, and back into the last signature. Repeat until you've sewn through all the holes in the back cover. Sew into the last signature one more time, and tie a knot (see detail photo, right). Now trim the ends.

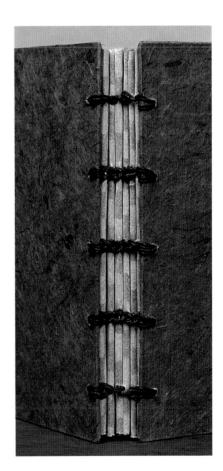

Fig. 7-17

Fig. 7-18

Variation
Elongated Coptic Stitch

Coptic is the stitch most frequently used for artists' books. The model is a single-needle stitch with hard covers, but a double-needle stitch with soft covers is easier. Try the elongated Coptic stitch with double threads. It's difficult to keep them parallel during the sewing, but the end result is worth it.

In simple Coptic stitch, you sew under the stitch before your last stitch. In elongated Coptic stitch, you skip the second-to-last stitch, and sew under the third-to-last stitch (see figure 7-19). This just makes the stitch one signature longer, but it has so much

more presence and beauty (see detail photo, bottom left).

This stitch is the most common of the traditional Coptic stitches used throughout history. It's so

dramatic and beautiful it makes me never want to sew simple Coptic again, even though simple

This model is another stub book. You can take advantage of the extra room afforded by a stub and tip in illustrations, such as the botanical prints on handmade paper used in this model (see detail photo, above).

Fig. 7-19

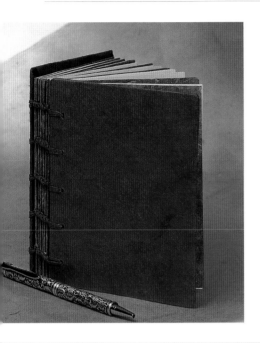

Variation

Twisted Coptic Stitch

This model is another traditional and historic Coptic binding.

Twisted Coptic is just simple Coptic with an extra stitch. I recommend using double threads for this and perhaps a heavier or thicker thread, like waxed linen. The stitch seems to want bulk.

Follow the instructions for simple Coptic stitch until you get the first chain stitch of the Coptic stitch. Make that stitch, sewing under the stitch before your last stitch. Next, stitch under the beginning of your last stitch, just before sewing back into the hole (see figure 7-20).

Fig. 7-20

BOOK MAPPING

When flipping through a book for the first time, you'll notice that the pages fall open naturally to certain places, such as the center fold, or the pages between two signatures. The content you normally see on these prominent pages (whether it's illustrations or text) is often the best or most important in a book. This doesn't happen by accident—it's the result of a process called *book mapping*. Book mapping allows you to adjust or adapt your content so that you can position your best work on the pages which will best display it.

There are as many different methods of book mapping as there are book designers. Here is the method I use:

Start your book mapping process with a single piece of paper (a regular piece of 8 ½ x 11-inch [21.6 x 27.9 cm] paper is fine). For each page that you plan to have in your book, attach a small removable note to the paper. Begin your model book with a single removable note, then continue with doubles, ending with a single again (see figure SB 7-1).

On each removable note, write an explanation of what will go on the page the note represents.

Looking at your schematic, identify all the pages which will open easily or automatically. Mark those places on your parent sheet (the paper on which you will print your actual book; see Glossary).

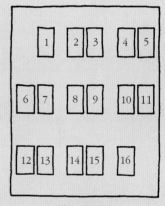

Fig. SB 7-1

Rearrange your removable notes as necessary. You may need to add to, adjust, or adapt your text or illustrations during this process to ensure that it gets the best placement possible.

Following your completed book map, proceed with your book, placing your best content in the correct positions marked on your parent sheet.

Book mapping can be a challenge, but it will improve the quality of your book, and is well worth it.

Gallery

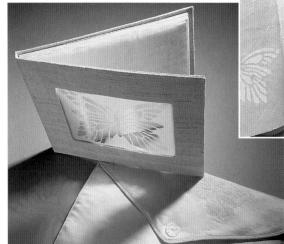

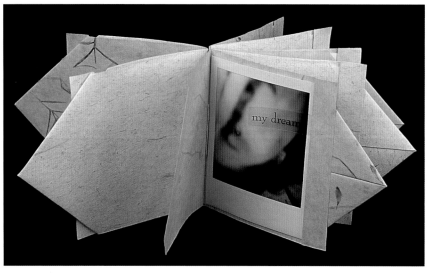

Top: Misty L. Youmans, *A Departure* (detail),1998. 8¾ x 11¼ inches (22.22 x 28.57 cm). Concertina spine with hinged pages and hard cover; Oriental and silk papers, mylar and silk organza; screen and ink jet printed, hand stencilled and gold leafed. Photo by Douglas Sandberg

Center: Peter Madden, *Garden Shadows*, 1999. 4½ x 14 inches (11.4 x 35.6 cm). Stab binding; cotton, paper, slate, copper and wood; dyed cyanotypes, solvent transfers, and embossing.

Left: Mia Semingson, *My Dreams*, 1999. 5.20 x 5¾ inches (13.2 x 14.6 cm). Origami folds and Coptic stitch; paper and acetate, color photos; ink jet printed.

Recessed Skewer Binding

This exposed binding technique is the result of a very bad illustration that I saw in a book. Misunderstanding what I saw, I thought the style featured a recessed skewer bound into a book. It was a happy accident, as this recessed skewer style resulted. The technique is especially good for two-signature books and for multisignature books with a center fold to display.

Evelyn Eller, *Victorian Alphabets*, 1998. 12 x 8 x 2 inches (30.5 x 20.3 x 5.1 cm). Painted hinged concertina; board, handmade and embossed paper, acetate; photocopied.

Single-Signature Recessed Skewer Binding

This is a very versatile style which can be altered into countless variations. There is no sewing required, and although the results look sophisticated, it's very easy to create.

SINGLE-SIGNATURE RECESSED SKEWER BINDING

Materials

4 pieces of text weight paper, 5¾ x 8½ inches (14.6 x 21.6 cm)

1 piece of pastel paper, 6 x 9 inches (15.2 x 22.9 cm)

1 piece of marbled paper, 4 x 4 inches (10.2 x 10.2 cm)

1 piece of marbled paper, 4¼ x 4¼ inches (10.795 x 10.795 cm)

2 bamboo skewers, each 6 inches (15.2 cm) long

2 ribbons, each 5⅛ inches (13 cm) long

Beads and dangling objects (optional)

Note: A hand-held hole punch is needed for this project.

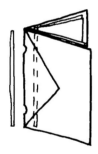

Fig. 8-1

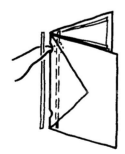

Fig. 8-2

Instructions

1 Fold each piece of text weight paper in half and nest them together in a signature.

2 Fold the small marbled paper in half diagonally, and wrap it around the signature.

3 Apply adhesive to the larger marbled square, and place it in the center of the pastel paper. When your adhesive dries, fold the pastel paper in half and nest your signature inside it.

4 Using a hand-held hole punch, punch a hole in both the head and tail of the signature and cover, about 1 inch (2.5 cm) in from the edges, or wherever is comfortable.

5 Place one skewer inside and one outside the signature, touching the spine (see figure 8-1 and detail photo below).

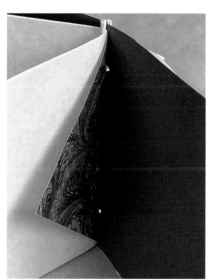

6 Thread a ribbon from the outside to the inside, around the inside skewer, and back out again. Place the outside skewer in the center of the ribbon and tie a knot, even if you want a bow (see figure 8-2). Bows come undone, and that would disbind your book. After the knot, tie a bow, tie on beads and dangling objects if you like, or make a braid.

7 Repeat the process for the other hole (see detail photo, below, right). If the skewers are too long, trim them using wire cutters (regular scissors aren't strong enough). Place the skewers inside a paper bag before you cut them with wire cutters or they will pop through the air.

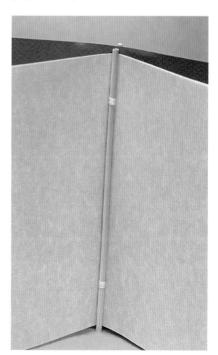

Variation

Two-Signature Recessed Skewer Book with Flap Covers

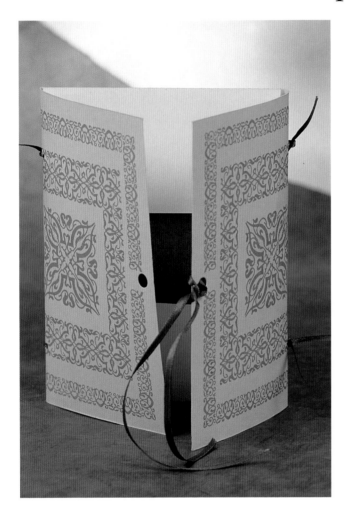

This model features a cover with two sets of flaps, vertical and horizonal, made from a single piece of paper. When the cover is opened, two signatures are revealed, each bound to the cover by a skewer. This design is a great way to present two books inside a single cover.

Create your cover from a single piece of cover weight paper. Cut, score, and fold two sets of flaps. The horizontal flaps will fold over and fit inside the vertical flaps when the book is closed. The folds inside the vertical flaps will be the book's spines.

Create two signatures and wrap them. Punch holes at the head and tail of the both your signatures. Punch a hole on either side of each spine fold at the head and the tail, corresponding to the holes in your signatures. The holes should be close to but not touching the fold.

Place a skewer inside each signature. Sew a ribbon from the outside, through one hole, around the skewer, and out the hole on the other side of the fold. Tie a knot. Repeat on the other pair of holes, and again for the other signature.

Punch a hole on the fore edge of each vertical cover flap. Thread a ribbon through the fore edge hole on one flap, and then through the corresponding hole on the other flap. Your book will tie closed in an arch shape.

SPECIMEN BOOKS

Specimen books are designed to showcase examples of a particular group of things; for example, paper, calligraphy, fonts, or illustrations. From the past to the present, artists have made specimen books to display their talents in calligraphy or to entice potential customers with the array of fabrics their shops produced. Since the invention of the printing press, specimen books have been used to showcase examples of all the fonts or papers available at a printer's shop. Type specimen pages display the alphabet in both lower and upper case, plus all the grammatical marks and numbers. An artists' specimen book can take the idea a step further. The content can be anything you wish.

If you have a computer, I recommend creating a type specimen book. You can use your pages to display all the fonts on your computer. Start with a paragraph of text rather than just individual letters, as type often looks different in text form. I also recommend creating a type chart for each font. Type the whole alphabet, numbers and symbols, in both lower and upper case. By

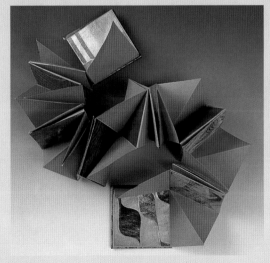

Barbara Selvidge, *Abstract to Zig Zap* (a paste paper specimen book), 1998. 3¼ x 3¼ inches (8.2 x 8.2 cm). Board, business and paste papers; Paste designs: methyl cellulose, fiber dye, pigment, mica.

simultaneously pressing the shift key and alt/option or shift/option keys (adjust the keys depressed according to your computer model), and then retyping all your keys, you'll reveal another layer of symbols that doesn't appear on your keyboard—a fascinating array of ornaments, ligatures, alternate letters, and expert fractions.

Another fun option for content is an illustration specimen book. Small private presses often create a specimen book to display illustrations in various media. Pick an image and create it in as many different media as possible (pencil, charcoal, pen and ink drawing, printmaking, block printing, mono printing, etc.), and on different kinds of paper. The results are generally amazing. If you are part of a class, you could create a collaborative illustration specimen book. Have everyone in the class do a couple of drawings and sign them, then photocopy everything so each person gets a copy. This is a great group project, and a great way to teach and learn new skills.

Variation

Two-Signature Recessed Skewer Book with Soft Covers

Prepare two signatures and wrap each with a soft cover. Using the hand-held hole punch, punch holes in both signatures at the head and tail. Place a skewer inside each signature (see detail photo, below left). Thread a ribbon from the outside into the first signature, around the skewer, and out. Repeat this for the second signature using the same ribbon (see figure 8-4). Snug up the ends, creating a tight tension. Tie a knot and repeat for the other hole. Finish with bows, beads and dangling objects, or braids, as you like (see detail photo, below right).

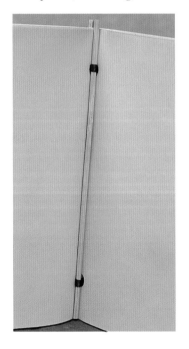

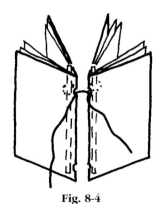

Fig. 8-4

This is model repeats the process used for a two-signature recessed skewer binding to form a six-signature book.

Follow the instructions for a two-signature recessed skewer binding on page 116, but instead of lining up all your holes, stagger the holes in the first and last signatures (see figure 8-8). The first and last signatures have only two holes each, placed relatively close together. The four remaining signatures (in the center) have four holes each; two line up with the holes in the first and last signatures, and the other two are placed further out, closer to the head and tail.

Your first signature is tied only to the second, through their corresponding holes. The second signature is attached to the third through the outer holes, and third to the

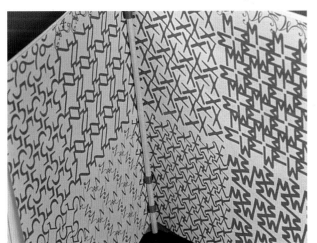

Variation
Multisignature Staggered Binding

fourth through the inner holes—they alternate. You'll have knots in different spots on spine; two on top, three in middle, three in second to last, and two on bottom.

With so many ends hanging loose off the spine, it becomes a riot of color, lengths, beads, and dangling objects.

Since each signature's center fold is displayed so well, a

typographic decorative paper with a design made up of letters combined in a pattern was used for visual interest (see detail photo, below left). Think of this binding as a display unit for your illustrations.

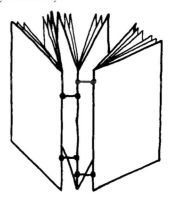

Fig. 8-8

Variation
Adding a Tunnel

This model takes the style a step further. Any time two pieces of heavy paper are next to each other you can add doors, windows, tunnels, and slipcases. A tunnel was added between the two signatures of this double-signature recessed skewer book (see detail photo, below left). Three layers were centered between the signatures. The outermost layer is a frame (with a cut-out center hole) which is folded around the fore edge of each signature's wrapper and then adhered in place. The next layer is adhered to the frame, and the innermost layer is adhered to the signature wrappers (see figure 8-5). Bows are tied on the outside (see detail photo, below).

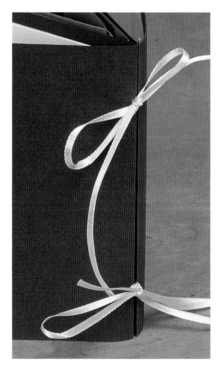

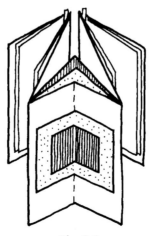

Fig. 8-5

EMBOSSING

Embossing describes the process of creating raised images or letters on paper. *Debossing* is the opposite; images or letters are pressed below the surface of the paper. Either effect can be achieved using wet or dry paper. It's a lot simpler than you might think—just follow the instructions below:

Note: Some papers work better than others for embossing. Commercial cover weight paper and many printmaking papers, are good examples. Ask for guidance at your art supply store. They might have a chart outlining different uses for papers. Thin papers tend not to emboss well. Stay away from rice papers and thin decorative papers because your embossing stylus will tear through them.

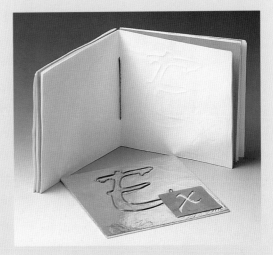

Shereen LaPlantz, *Spaces/Faces/Type: Illustrations*, 1997. 5½ x 5¾ inches (14 x 14.60 cm). Simple Coptic stitch; printmaking and business papers; screen and laser printed, wet embossed. Mold: Copper wire and saw-cut brass, glued onto board covered in aluminum foil.

DRY EMBOSSING

Start with a 10-point stock paper or an ordinary file folder. Cut a stencil of the image you wish to emboss.

Tape the stencil to a light table or window, then tape the paper you want to emboss over the stencil. Using the large end of your stylus, simply run the stylus around the inside of the stencil's cuts.

Sharpen the embossed image by repeating this process with the small end of the stylus. That's all there is to it. The trick is that you must be able to see light through the paper, which means dark-colored and heavy papers won't work.

To add color to your image, turn over the embossed paper. Place it on a flat surface, then place the stencil over the embossing. Stencil brush on a color using acrylic paint, watercolors, or rubber stamp inks. Everything will line up perfectly because you're using the same stencil.

WET EMBOSSING

Select an image that you wish to emboss. You can use objects such as paper clips, pine needles, wooden or metal found objects, or cut a stencil out of a four-ply museum board, heavy mat board, or any other noncorrugated cardboard.

Select a heavy paper and wet it by placing it in a plastic tray filled with water. I recommend soaking the paper for about 30 seconds. Have a bath towel close by, and blot off the big drops of water.

Place the paper over the object or stencil, and apply pressure. You can use your thumbs, hammer the paper with a rubber mallet, or run the paper and stencil through a printing press. Let the paper dry, and it's embossed.

If a crisper emboss is desired, and a press is not available, try using male and female stencils. Place the wet paper over the male stencil and press the female portion in place.

Letters can be difficult to hand cut into a stencil. Ask your local trophy shop to cut letters for you in metal or plastic. Since these shops are used to doing engraving, not stencils, they seem incredulous that you want to cut all the way through on purpose. Assure them that this is indeed what you want. You can get whole paragraphs engraved into stencils for embossing.

Multisignature Recessed Skewer with a Twisted Coptic Stitch

Combine techniques like a mix-and-match wardrobe. Consider which styles suit a book's theme, and use them together. For this model, a multisignature recessed skewer binding was combined with the twisted Coptic stitch.

1 Create as many signatures as you want (the model has six). Fold four pieces of text weight paper in half for each. Create a wrapper from cover weight paper for each.

2 Poke two holes in each signature (near the head and tail), and corresponding holes in the wrappers.

3 Nest each signature in a wrapper and place a skewer inside it.

4 Using a waxed linen thread, sew in either of the first signature's holes, going around the skewer and coming back out (see figure 8-6).

5 Repeat the process, adding the next signature and sewing in its corresponding hole. When you come to the third signature, start the Coptic stitch (see steps 8-15, page 100-102). Sew under not your last stitch, but the one before it.

6 To make the twist, sew under the first part of the Coptic stitch (see figure 7-20 on page 109) and continue on to the next signature (see figure 8-7).

7 When you get to the last signature, tie a knot in the end of your thread. Go back and do this at the beginning of your thread, too. Trim your ends.

8 Repeat this process on the other row of holes.

The front of each of the signature wrappers is embossed as, described on page 119.

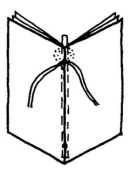

Fig. 8-6

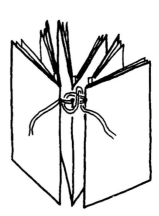

Fig. 8-7

EPHEMERA, BROADSIDES, EPIGRAMS, AND CATCHPENNY PRINTS

The word *ephemera* implies something that's not meant to last. Postage stamps, playbills, postcards, promotional folders, and greeting cards are some examples of printed ephemera (see photo, below center). Since the printed ephemera you create probably won't be saved, it's a good opportunity to try new stuff. I've printed and bound my workshop prospectus' and my New Year's cards. The card in the center of the photo on the right is my first attempt at writing humor.

A *broadside* is a single sheet of paper that states an opinion—usually an inflammatory one. Broadsides started out as the last words of condemned prisoners and were posted next to the gallows for one day. During the Revolutionary War in the United States, broadsides were used to promote the Revolution. The example shown on the left in the photo above is a quote, so it's not a true broadside.

Shereen LaPlantz, *Broadside, Card, Catchpenny Print.*

Epigrams are short statements or quotes, such as the ones I've used: "Be Creative" or "Illuminate Your Life." A hundred years ago they were often sold as wall plaques and were a part of most fine printer's catalogs. Today it's still possible to create a poster-size epigram, but you may want to try making one that fits on an artists' stamp.

Catchpenny prints were, and still are, educational prints for children. They were initially very small images that form a border around a horn book (a child's learning tablet). Today, they are usually posters. Catchpenny prints are typically composed of many images, not necessarily on the same subject. One in my collection shows a king, an Eskimo, a bluebird, a lion, the Taj Mahal, a castle, and more. You may want to use clip art to save time.

Gail S. Looper, *Rock 'n Roll Honey*, 1997. 7 x 17 inches (17.8 x 43.2 cm). Flag book binding; paper and concert tickets. Photo by John Lucas.

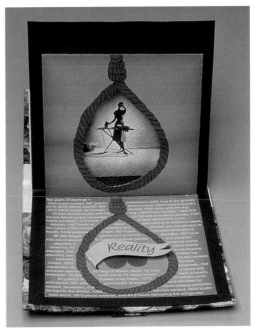

Top left: Michael Jacobs, *Towers*, 1999. 4 x 7½ x ¾ inches (10.2 x 19.1 x 1.9 cm). Concertina, closed; pre-printed paper, mixed media, brass fleur-de-lis.

Top right: Betsy Dollar, *Diary*, 1999. 6½ x 5½ inches (16.5 x 14 cm). Glued binding, pastel and business papers, cut; ink jet printed. Photo by Geoffrey Wheeler

Right: Susan Hensel, *Concrete Canyons*, 1998. 11 x 17 inches (27.9 x 43.2 cm). Hinged concertina, closed: board & lig-free board; acrylic painting. Photo by Kim Kauffman

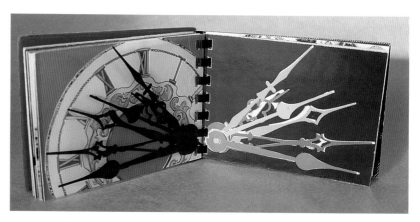

Top left: Charles Hobson, *Fresnel's Tower*, 1997. 6 x 5¼ x 5¼ inches (15.2 x 13.33 x 13.33 cm). Case binding, closed; boards, fabric, mirror paper; photogravure etching.

Top right: Gloria Helfgott, *An Herbal*, 1998. 5 inch hexagon (12.7 cm). Pamphlet stitch; boards, leather, printmaking paper; calligraphy & acrylic painting.

Above: Jill Timm, *Watch Book*, 1973. 4¼ x 6 inches (10.79 x 15.2 cm). Specimen book of various ways to show a watch; comb binding; acetate, paper and mixed media, photography; collage, markers, ink, and gouache; screen printed.

Left: Marcia Buch, *My Grandmother's House*, 1997. 7 x 12 inches (17.8 x 30.5 cm). Board and pastel paper, sewn over tapes; colored pencil and ink jet printed.

CONTRIBUTING ARTISTS

JODY ALEXANDER
FELTON, CA

TRACY APLIN
BERKELEY, CA

PAM BARTON
VOLCANO, HI

ELAINE S. BENJAMIN
BLUE LAKE, CA

WADETH BORY
BAYSIDE, CA

JEANNE WHITFIELD BRADY
SMITHVILLE, TN

MARCIA BUCH
CANTON, CT

DIANE CASSIDY
CUPERTINO, CA

CATHY DeFOREST
LAFAYETTE, CA

MELISSA DINWIDDIE
ENLO PARK, CA

BETSY DOLLAR
BOULDER, CO

DAYLE DOROSHOW
BRISBANE, CA

EVELYN ELLER
FOREST HILLS, NY

DOROTHY FENN
MISSION VIEJO, CA

JULIE FRIEDMAN
MEDINA, OH

C. J. GROSSMAN
SAN FRANSICO, CA

MARTHA HALL
ORR'S ISLAND, ME

GLORIA HELFGOTT
PACIFIC PALISADES, CA

SUSAN HENSEL
EAST LANSING, MI

CHARLES HOBSON
STINSON BEACH, CA

DIANE PERIN HOCK
HEALDSBURG, CA

JUDITH HOFFMAN
SAN MATEO, CA

MICHAEL JACOBS
SEATTLE, WA

MARCY JOHNSON
SEATTLE, WA

SUSAN KAPUSCINSKI GAYLORD
NEWBURYPORT, MA

MITZI LINDGREN
BELLINGHAM, WA

VIVIANA LOMBROZO
LA JOLLA, CA

GAIL S. LOOPER
SMITHVILLE, TN

PETER MADDEN
BOSTON, MA

DEBRA MADISON
SACRAMENTO, CA

JONE SMALL MANOOGIAN
PALO ALTO, CA

EMILY MARTIN
IOWA CITY, IA

DIANE MAURER-MATHISON
SPRING MILLS, PA

CATHERINE MICHAELIS
VASHON ISLAND, WA

SUSAN MERRITT
SAN DIEGO, CA

JACKIE MORSE
THE SEA RANCH, CA

KAREN PAGE
PORT TOWNSEND, WA

LYNNE PERRELLA
ANCRAM, NY

HELEN PETRE
JULIAN, CA

RUTH PETTY
CLACKAMAS, OR

JoANNA POEHLMANN
MILWAUKEE, WI

JAN OWEN
BANGOR, ME

SUSAN ROTOLO
NEW YORK, NY

GENIE SHENK
SOLANA BEACH, CA

ALICE SIMPSON
NEW YORK, NY

BARBARA SELVIDGE
SAN FRANCISO, CA

MIA SEMINGSON
LOUISVILLE, CO

JOAN M. SOPPE
CEDAR RAPIDS, IA

R.H. STARR, JR.
OWINGS MILL, MD

DOROTHY SWENDEMAN
EUREKA, CA

LIZ TAMAYO
OAKLAND, CA

DEDICATED TO

Tracy Aplin, my binding assistant, who jumped in and helped me while I had cancer, and once again with the models for this book when I had a mastectomy. Thanks, Tracy!

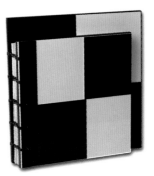

David LaPlantz, my husband, who supports me in every endeavor. He didn't just stand by me during the cancer, he almost picked me up and carried me through it. Thanks, and all my love Honey!

Above right: Tracy Aplin, *Matrix*, 1997. 6 x 6 inches (15.2 x 15.2 cm). Board, anodized aluminum chain mail, pen and ink drawings.

Above left: David LaPlantz, *Black and White: A Cultural Odyssey*, 2000. 8 x 8 x 1 inches (20.3 x 20.3 x 2.5 cm). Elongated Coptic stitch for stub binding; fiberboard, painted and engraved aluminum, lokta and business papers; ink jet printed.

ACKNOWLEDGMENTS

This book was more of a collaborative effort than usual because I underwent a mastectomy during the process of writing it. I'm especially thankful to Tracy Aplin who made the models and illustrations in the book when I couldn't. Also, special thanks to Carla Tenret, who did the calligraphy for the chapter titles. A collaborative project is special because it shows each person's strengths.

I would also like to acknowledge two people who made the environment ready for me to enter. Hedi Kyle has encouraged and promoted book arts for decades, helping the field to reach its current popularity. Keith Smith, through his book *Non-Adhesive Binding*, let me know that visual creativity in books had gone beyond the covers and illustrations. He started me on this journey.

Thank you, all of you.

INDEX

Colophon

The text for this book was set in 10-point Garamond. This font is based on the designs of the sixteenth-century printer, publisher, and type designer Claude Garamond. His designs were modeled on type made by Venetian printers at the end of the fifteenth century. The chapter titles in this book were done by hand in calligraphy by Carla Tenret. This book was created with Quark Express on a Power Mac G4/4000. The book was printed by Oceanic Graphic Printing Productions, Ltd. in China on 128 gsm Japanese matte art paper.